Horace *Odes*

T0331531

The following titles are available from Bloomsbury for the OCR specifications in Latin and Greek for examinations from June 2019 to June 2021

Apuleius *Metamorphoses* V: A Selection, with introduction, commentary notes and vocabulary by Stuart R. Thomson

Cicero *Philippic* II: A Selection, with introduction, commentary notes and vocabulary by Christopher Tanfield

Horace *Odes:* A Selection, with introduction, commentary notes and vocabulary by John Godwin

Horace *Satires:* A Selection, with introduction, commentary notes and vocabulary by John Godwin

Ovid *Amores* II: A Selection, with introduction, commentary notes and vocabulary by Alfred Artley

Tacitus *Histories* I: A Selection, with introduction by Ellen O'Gorman and commentary notes and vocabulary by Benedict Gravell

Virgil *Aeneid* XI: A Selection, with introduction, commentary notes and vocabulary by Ashley Carter

OCR Anthology for Classical Greek AS and A Level, covering the prescribed texts by Aristophanes, Euripides, Herodotus, Homer, Plato and Xenophon, with introduction, commentary notes and vocabulary by Stephen P. Anderson, Rob Colborn, Neil Croally, Charlie Paterson, Chris Tudor and Claire Webster

Supplementary resources for these volumes can be found at
www.bloomsbury.com/OCR-editions-2019-2021
Please type the URL into your web browser and follow
the instructions to access the Companion Website.
If you experience any problems, please
contact Bloomsbury at academicwebsite@bloomsbury.com

Horace *Odes*:
A Selection

Odes III.2, III.3, III.4, III.6

With introduction, commentary
notes and vocabulary
by John Godwin

BLOOMSBURY ACADEMIC
LONDON • NEW YORK • OXFORD • NEW DELHI • SYDNEY

BLOOMSBURY ACADEMIC
Bloomsbury Publishing Plc
50 Bedford Square, London, WC1B 3DP, UK

BLOOMSBURY, BLOOMSBURY ACADEMIC and the
Diana logo are trademarks of Bloomsbury Publishing Plc

First published in Great Britain 2018

A catalogue record for this book is available from the British Library.

Library of Congress Cataloging-in-Publication Data
Names: Horace, author. | Godwin, John, 1955- editor.
Title: Odes : a selection odes 3.2, 3.3, 3.4, 3.6 / Horace ; with introduction,
commentary notes and vocabulary by John Godwin.
Description: London : Bloomsbury Academic, 2018. |
Includes bibliographical references.
Identifiers: LCCN 2017051802 | ISBN 9781501324222 (pbk.) |
ISBN 9781350000834 (epdf)
Subjects: LCSH: Horace–Criticism and interpretation.
Classification: LCC PA6393.C3 2018 | DDC 874/.01–dc23
LC record available at https://lccn.loc.gov/2017051802

ISBN: PB: 978-1-5013-2422-2
          ePDF: 978-1-3500-0083-4
          eBook: 978-1-3500-0084-1

Typeset by Integra Software Services Pvt. Ltd.

To find out more about our authors and books visit www.bloomsbury.com
and sign up for our newsletters.

Contents

Preface

This book is intended to assist students preparing for public examinations in Latin who are required to study this text, but it can of course be used by any students of Latin who have mastered the basics and who are now ready to start reading some Latin verse and developing their skills and their understanding. The notes assume that the reader has studied the Latin language roughly as far as GCSE, but the vocabulary list glosses every word in the text and the Introduction assumes that the reader is coming to Horace for the first time. Tricky phrases are explained and translated in the commentary; and, to assist with the comprehension of the Latin, the vocabulary at the end of the book often includes line references to places where a particular word has a different meaning from the one found in basic dictionaries, and it is worth consulting the vocabulary whenever the meaning is not fully explained in the commentary to be certain of the meaning of every word. In this way the music and the emphases of the verse can be more fully appreciated. The commentary seeks to elucidate the background and the literary features of this highly artistic text, while also helping the reader to understand how the Latin words fit together into their sentences.

My thanks are due above all to Alice Wright and her team at Bloomsbury who have been a model of efficiency and enthusiasm and a delight to write for. My thanks also go to Professor Roland Mayer, of King's College, London and the anonymous readers (from Bloomsbury and from OCR) who read the whole of this book in draft form and made many highly useful comments which saved me from error as well as pointing me towards a better reading of the text.

John Godwin
Shrewsbury 2017

Introduction

Horace's *Odes*

This mosaic of words, in which every word, as sound, as place, as concept, streams out its strength right and left and over the whole; here the minimum, in terms of the range and number of the signs, achieves the maximum in the energy of the signs. All this is Roman and, if you will believe me, noble par excellence. All other poetry becomes, in comparison, something too popular, merely sentimental chattering. (Nietzsche, *Götzen-Dämmerung*)

Horace published *Odes* books I–III as a single collection of poems in 23 BC. As a poetic achievement it ranks alongside the very best literature ever written and it certainly shows the poet to have been a master of his poetic craft. The eighty-eight poems in the three books are composed in lyric metres – many in the metres named after the great Greek lyric poets Sappho and Alcaeus, but also making use of other verse forms. The opening nine poems of the first book are all composed in different metres and his mastery of the complex rhythms is astonishing.

These are not merely technical exercises, however, and the poems also convey a kaleidoscope of social, political and personal situations. They cover love poems, party poems, poems to say *bon voyage* and poems to say 'welcome home', invitations, expressions of condolence, nature poems, hymns to the gods, political poems (sometimes explicit and sometimes (e.g. I.14) allegorical), philosophical musings and so on. Like all poems they are composed for performance and with a voice which may or may not express the feelings of the person writing the words. They are literary artefacts which often refer to other poetry and which thus invite the audience to judge the extent to which they are ironic. Many of the odes are addressed to named people and so may be targeted at the known proclivities of the person addressed – be it the *bon viveur* Maecenas invited to drink cheap wine in *Odes* I.20 or else the girl Lalage (whose name means 'chatterbox' in Greek) being described (I.22.24) as 'talking sweetly'. Poems sometimes start off in one vein and end up in another: 1.9 starts as a nature poem describing winter and moves naturally into a recommendation to stay warm indoors and then into a meditation on enjoying life in the face of an uncertain future.

The opening six odes of the third book are usually referred to as the 'Roman Odes': they are unusual in the collection in that they are all composed in the same verse form (Alcaics) and all are explicitly political. These lengthy poems do not have named addressees (poem 6 is addressed to *Romane* but no specific Roman is ever named) and there is little or no light relief in the form of lighter topics mingled into the politics. They are also difficult to interpret as the poet's attitude towards the Augustan themes of austerity, courage, devotion to the gods and moral high standards is not always clear, conveyed as it is in verse which is strongly reminiscent of its Greek predecessors and which can at times sound like ironic pastiche rather than simply heart-on-sleeve praise. Poem 3, for instance, begins with Stoic generalities recording the immortality granted to great men and leads to a version of the speech purported to have been given by the goddess Juno allowing the deification of Romulus but also demanding that Troy may not be rebuilt: the poem ends with an ironic twist as the poet addresses his Muse and asks her to stop using the 'lowly' form of lyric for lofty epic themes such as this.

These are not, then, simple poems, but they repay repeated study. If the *Odes* represent the finest lyric produced by the Romans, then the

336 lines of the 'Roman Odes' must surely rank as the finest sustained piece of political poetry produced by this highly political society.

The life of Horace

Quintus Horatius Flaccus was born on 8 December 65 BC in Venusia in southern Italy, the son of an ex-slave as he tells us himself (e.g. *Satires* I.6.6). His father was clearly a man of some means with his own land and a job as a *coactor* (auctioneering manager): he was rich enough to send young Horace to be schooled in Rome and then to university in Athens, which is where the young poet was in 44 BC when the news of Caesar's assassination broke. Horace joined up with the forces of Brutus, one of the leading assassins, and became a *tribunus militum* (senior officer). He fought for Brutus at the battle of Philippi in 42 BC where the republicans were defeated. He returned to Rome and managed to secure employment as a clerk to the treasury (*scriba quaestorius*), which is somewhat surprising in view of his fighting on the 'wrong' side in the war. He was a friend of the poet Virgil and through him was introduced to Maecenas who was one of Octavian's leading advisers and a patron of the arts. Under his patronage, Horace was introduced to Octavian himself and was even (it is said) offered a job as a secretary with him – a job he refused. After a few years he obtained a small Sabine farm in the hillside near Rome, probably as a result of the patronage of Maecenas.

He began his writing career with the *Epodes* and the two books of *Satires*, all published in the 30s BC: poems which are forthright and at times outrageous to modern ears but which express the spirit of frank outspokenness which was prized in the Roman Republic and which we also see in the work of such republican poets as Lucilius and Catullus. In the 20s BC he worked on the first three books of *Odes* which appeared in 23 BC. He followed this with the first book of *Epistles,* a form of light didactic verse purporting to be letters and containing philosophy and some satirical content. His most public commission was to compose the *Carmen Saeculare* for the 'Secular Games' in 17 BC, which was all part of the emperor Augustus' celebration of the national revival under his rule. Horace composed a fourth book of *Odes* and some more verse epistles – one of them addressed to the emperor personally. He died in 8 BC, not long after the death of his patron Maecenas.

Horace and Augustus

Horace's career therefore spanned what has been called 'the Roman revolution' (a term made famous by Ronald Syme's 1939 history of the period in a book of that name). When he was born the republic was being governed by the Senate and People of Rome and the army commanders such as Pompey and Caesar were (in theory) simply carrying out the wishes of the state in attacking foreign enemies such as the pirates in 67 BC and Mithridates (in 66–62 BC). All this changed when Julius Caesar was governing the province of Gaul and was unable to return to Rome without facing political ruin from his enemies in the senate: on 10 January 49 BC he famously crossed the river Rubicon (the stream which divided his province from the rest of the world and was the boundary of his military authority). He thus effectively marched his troops against their fatherland in an act of civil war. This war brought about the dictatorship of Caesar which ended when he was assassinated on 15 March 44 BC.

The period from 44–31 BC was one of turmoil and uncertainty. The forces loyal to the dead dictator – led by Mark Antony, who was Caesar's consul, and Octavian, who was Caesar's heir – fought a series of wars against the republicans who had killed Caesar. Octavian, Antony and Lepidus formed the second triumvirate after the crushing of the republicans and carried out proscriptions which amounted to a purge of Caesar's opponents, including the great orator and statesman Cicero who lost his life in 43 BC. Lepidus disappeared from the scene, and shortly afterwards Antony and Octavian divided their powers into separate spheres, with Antony forming an eastern power-base in Egypt alongside the queen Cleopatra while Octavian ruled the western Mediterranean. The rivalry between them came to a climax in the sea battle off Actium in Greece on 2 September 31 BC. Antony and Cleopatra were defeated, leaving Octavian the undisputed master of the Roman world at the age of 31. He returned to Rome in 29 BC and in January 27 BC he was given the title of 'Augustus' and the position of *princeps*.

This was uncharted territory in Roman politics. They had had kings in the distant past – the last one was Tarquin the Proud who was expelled in 509 BC. They had also had dictators such as Sulla who was ruthless towards his enemies and died of natural causes, and recently Caesar who was clement towards his enemies and was assassinated. Augustus had to find a path whereby he could rule without seeming to be a ruler. In his account of his achievements (*Res Gestae*) he tells us that he only acted as the senate told him and that he in fact 'liberated Rome from the tyranny of a faction', although this is obviously not the whole truth. He took constitutional offices such as the consulship and later adopted tribunician power as the 'term of the highest power' (*summi fastigii vocabulum* (Tacitus *Annals* III.56)). Augustus was clearly determined to avoid the Scylla of tyranny and the Charybdis of political insignificance. Augustus promoted a vision of Roman values which included clemency to his enemies but he was wise enough not to let this prevent him executing or exiling any perceived threats to his regime, such as was to happen to the poet Ovid in AD 8. The major part of Augustus' appeal was to the sense of shared values which Romans had, and above all to the feeling that life was immeasurably better under the peace and prosperity of an emperor than it had been in the almost chaotic days of the dying republic. His title 'Augustus' suggested the sort of 'awe' which was inspired by the divine and is something to bear in mind when reading Horace's pronouncements on the future divinity of the emperor.

One specific area which is highlighted in the Roman Odes is that of the Parthians. In 53 BC the Roman general Crassus was defeated by them at the battle of Carrhae with the deaths of 20,000 men and the loss of the Roman legionary standards. This disgrace needed to be avenged and the standards needed to be recovered, and Romans were keen and confident that Augustus would succeed in doing this where Antony had failed in 36 BC. Horace refers to this several times in these poems (II.3, III.44, VI.9–10) and it was clearly part of the Augustan agenda to safeguard the border with the Parthian empire. In fact, he did so by diplomacy and the threat of invasion rather than by overt warfare and secured the return of the standards (and some Roman prisoners who had been held since 53 BC) in 20 BC. Horace was composing his poems in the heady early days of the regime when such projects were objectives and fuel for both patriotism and also restoring Roman pride. The poet neatly expresses the view that all this was both right and proper even in the age of self-proclaimed 'Augustan peace'.

In these poems, then, the poet speaks to and for his community in a given political situation. When the poet appears to be mouthing the sentiments of his government or praising the emperor, is this toadying propaganda and selling out to the regime? What would the 23-year-old Horace, fighting for the republic, have made of the 43-year-old author of these *Odes*? There is no single simple answer to this question – which is also fired at Virgil's *Aeneid* albeit in different ways – but some thoughts may help to promote further discussion.

Horace's earliest works (the *Epodes* and *Satires*) were mostly poems of critical judgement, sometimes excessively so. Many readers come to the *Odes* and see these too as pieces expressing value judgements, composed in a spirit of gratitude to the new *princeps* for the renewal of the economy, the land and the values of old Italy. Anyone who had lived through the wars and shortages of the last century BC would no doubt feel thankful and optimistic now that the new regime was in power with its apparent offer of peace and new hope. This aspect of the poetry should not be curtly dismissed. For one thing, this relationship is not solely one of subordination to new masters. Horace mentions (IV.26) the battle of Philippi and does not apologise for being on the 'wrong' side there, and clearly feels that he enjoys security and status as a *vates*, and therefore speaks as some sort of spokesman to and for the regime. It is also worth pointing out that Augustus laid great store by the value of *clementia* ('forgiveness' of enemies) and so Horace could be positively advertising this Augustan value in his mention of Philippi (for which see especially *Odes* II.7). Horace's sententious moralising (such as poem VI) can seem subservient support for the new social legislation – but it could also be seen to be offering advice and encouragement to a man eager to bring in moral and social legislation and not yet able to do so. Augustus (63 BC–AD 14) had only begun to rule in the early 20s BC and Horace was therefore writing for a relatively inexperienced ruler. Poetry such as this acts as a mirror of the regime in which the government may see itself – and popular sentiments – reflected. Mirrors are not usually flattering.

Throughout the ancient world there were examples of powerful men having a 'wise man' to offer advice and thought – Scipio with his Laelius, for instance, or Nero with his Seneca. The tradition whereby poetry was seen as an ethical force for good is as old as Homer himself – Agamemnon left a 'bard' with his wife Clytemnestra when he went to Troy in a (futile) bid to maintain her wifely fidelity (*Odyssey* III.267–8), and Roman poets had something of a habit of dedicating their poems to men of legal and/or political action (as Horace addresses *Satires* II.1 to Trebatius, as Lucretius' patron was Memmius, or Tibullus with his patron Valerius Messalla Corvinus). This relationship went both ways, however. The tradition of 'panegyric' was strong in ancient poetry, stretching from Pindar's choral lyrics to celebrate the victories of athletes in the games right up to the last pagan poet of Imperial Rome, Claudian, with his epics in honour of the great and powerful of his day. The father of Roman literature, Ennius, was much in demand as a writer who could praise famous men, according to Cicero (*pro Archia* XXII); there was a strong urge from the men of action to have a bard to immortalize their exploits in literary form, a form of immortality which Horace is alive to:

> vixere fortes ante Agamemnona
> multi; sed omnes inlacrimabiles
> urgentur ignotique longa
> nocte, carent quia vate sacro. (*Odes* IV.9, 25–8)
> (many brave men lived before Agamemnon, but all are unwept, unknown and pressed down by long night, because they had no inspired poet.)

Did this mean that Horace was a court poet working for 'Caesar who was able to compel' (*Caesar qui cogere posset* (*Satires* I.3.4))? Several of the Augustan poets claim that they are not up to the task of composing the military epic which the regime is asking of them and this 'refusal poem' or *recusatio* became something of a genre in itself (*Odes* I.6, II.12, *Satires* II.1.12–15, Virgil *Eclogues* VI.3–5, Propertius II.1). This could easily become ironic as the poet composes a poem saying what he is *not* going to write about, allowing him to have his cake and eat it – something like the irony of *Epode* II where lengthy praise of the country life is ended with the revelation that the speaker is an incorrigible townie ('any day now going to live in the country'). Military epic was nothing new, of course, and the search for originality would not find much hope of satisfaction in yet another epic celebrating yet another battle: it might have seemed easy to a skilled poet to 'do' epic like this, but in fact it would have been almost impossible to create original poetry on so hackneyed a theme. Virgil succeeded magnificently, of course, in his epic *The Aeneid* which was being composed as Horace wrote his *Odes* I–III. There was no room for two men tackling the same idea.

Horace's choice of lyric form for his political poetry was a master stroke in itself. The idea of marrying the public issues of the day with the private form of the lyric is not totally original – his Greek model Alcaeus had done this, as we will see – but it had not been done before in Latin and the artistic licence of the lyric is invaluable in creating the *persona* of the inspired poet/public speaker. The *Odes* with their Greek background mix together the Greek and the Roman, the past and the present and future, the topical and everyday and the dark reaches of myth and legend. They claim to be works of art whose primary loyalty is to the Muses rather than the government, but the poems in this book are certainly related to the issues of the day.

They make use of political topics but the poems are not reducible to party political broadcasts, any more than Virgil's *Aeneid* is just a sop to Augustus. The form of the poems – the lyric metres and the high-flown language, for instance – make it harder to take the content at face value. If a modern political party were to make an opera out of their manifesto, we would not simply listen to the words but would feel that something more than mere political narratives was going on. Lyric, with its pretence of musical accompaniment and use of exotic metres, allows elements of fantasy and imagination which would be hard to sustain in satire or even epic. There are moments in the *Odes* (as there are in Virgil) where the praise element seems overblown and the whiff of irony can be detected or suspected: here again the poet can retreat into the fantasy world of poetry, but here too he can be seen to be showing the emperor the awesome imagery which the public expect of him. If Augustus is seen in mythical terms ('drinking nectar amongst the gods' (III.12)) then that is a burden for the ruler to bear, a set of expectations for him to match as well as praise for what he is achieving.

One could try to interpret the poems as in some ways anti-Augustan, sneering in sarcastic praise and embarrassing the ruler with extravagant and absurd praise, but this is a judgement which few people would make. When Horace refers to Augustus' second wife Livia (herself divorced from her first husband) as *unico gaudens mulier marito* (III.14.5: 'a woman rejoicing in her one and only husband') this could sound like sarcasm; but the myth of Livia the model wife was one which the whole of Rome swallowed when this mother of two was granted the 'right of three children' and once again it is more tempting to see the poet here mirroring the emotion of the times rather than having a dig at the powerful. Readers will judge for themselves as they read these poems whether they are tongue in cheek – or heart on sleeve, or somewhere in between.

The issues are complex and cannot be simplified while doing them justice. The literary world of Horace is one influenced strongly by the Greek poet Callimachus whose proclaimed objective of *l'art pour l'art*, whose love of the small-scale and abhorrence of the bombastic, whose quest for perfection in form all shine through the *Odes* of Horace. The poet was perhaps trying to have it both ways in seeking to be a spokesman for the great with the voice of the private citizen: to be the aesthetic artist with a public *persona*. In a crude sense, Horace the Epicurean can enjoy peace and quiet precisely because Caesar is in charge and takes care of the threats for him, as the poet readily admits in III.14 and IV.15.17–20: but Epicureanism, which lends itself more readily to monarchy than Stoicism ever would, is only part of the poet's philosophical armour (see below on 'The philosophical background'). In literary terms these poems cannot be reduced or seen as simply propaganda. Horace seems to mythologize the emperor, but then he also mythologizes himself in III.4 and the style effects something of an ironic distance which makes crude interpretation impossible. In short, as Lowrie (*Horace's Narrative Odes* 259) asks aptly, 'Who is in charge? in the realm of history, Augustus clearly is, but in the realm of poetry it is the poet – even in political matters.'

One thing seems certain, the *Odes*, like Virgil's *Aeneid*, are a part of the Augustan regime which they celebrate. They represent the appropriation of Greece into the Roman world in literature just as the state itself had taken the lands of Greece into the Roman Empire. Horace is in this sense a conqueror of poetic 'territory', just as Epicurus is praised by Lucretius (I.72–9) in quasi-military terms for *his* conquering of the world through his philosophy. There is huge pride here – most obviously in III.30, where the imagery of a poetic memorial 'more enduring than bronze and higher than ... the pyramids' is almost a snub to the emperor whose own memorials are thereby made inferior. The poet has foreseen the deification of the emperor (e.g. III.11–12) and here at the end of the book foretells the immortality of his work and his own partial immortality as a result: *non omnis moriar* ('I shall not die completely'). *Odes* III.30 is (as often) a 'sealing' poem to close the book (cf. *Epistles* I.20 for a similar effect) – and it shows a literary pride which in its own way aspires to match (and even outdo?) the achievements of the regime which allowed it the air with which to sing.

The lyric poem in Greece and Rome

Graecia capta ferum victorem cepit et artes
intulit agresti Latio (*Epistles* II.1.156–7)
'Captured Greece captured her fierce conqueror and brought the
    arts to rustic Latium.'

vos exemplaria Graeca
nocturna versate manu, versate diurna (*Ars Poetica* 268–9)
'turn over the Greek models by night and by day.'

Horace may have felt that he was breaking new ground and mastering Greek forms for the Roman world, but his words quoted above show that the mastery was reciprocated and it is good to recall that Latin literature was in many ways parasitic on the Greek genres and literary works which inspired it. Would there have been an *Aeneid* without a Homer? Certainly not the sort of *Aeneid* we have; and it is almost certain that the *Odes* of Horace would not have existed in their metre and language without a Greek tradition of lyric poetry to inspire them.

Greek lyric poetry was one of the great literary achievements of the ancient world and it is a great pity that so little of this work survives. The nine great poets were named as: Alcman, Alcaeus, Anacreon, Bacchylides, Ibycus, Pindar, Sappho, Simonides and Stesichorus – who all flourished in the period from the seventh to the fifth centuries BC. The surviving work of the earlier poets is personal lyric, sung by a solo voice in short stanzas of the same metrical form. Later poets continued to compose personal lyric, but poets like Simonides, Bacchylides and Pindar also composed choral poetry, sung by choirs to the accompaniment of a lyre and often also of an *aulos* (a single-reed wind instrument something like a cross between an oboe and a recorder). The choral lyrics of this kind were usually composed in triadic form – two stanzas of identical metre followed by a third in a different but related rhythm. The personal lyric of an Alcaeus is associated with the party world of the symposium, whereas choral lyric suited public occasions such as religious ceremonies and especially the public celebration of an athletic victory at one of the major games in Greece.

The poems of Horace contained in this book are all composed in the metre named after the Greek lyric poet Alcaeus. Alcaeus was an aristocrat from the island of Lesbos who used his lyrical poetry to oppose the rule of the tyrant Pittacus with a combination of personal attack and some political comment. His was an age (seventh sixth centuries BC) when tyrants were springing up all over the Greek world and where political systems were constantly in a state of flux, epitomied in his famous image (fragment 6: cf. Horace *Odes* I.14) of the 'ship of state' tossed in the waves of unrest. His poetic themes are those of the aristocratic lifestyle of the age – love, drinking, warfare, politics and the values of the upper classes. He admits at one point to throwing away his shield to save himself in battle, and he enjoyed the pleasures of love and food; and we come away with the impression that his poems are in some sense an appeal to preserve and commemorate the way of life which he enjoyed.

Horace claims in the final poem of *Odes* III (30) that he would be said to have been 'the first man to have brought Aeolian song to Italian measures' (XXX.13–14: cf. *Epistles* I.19.32–3). He was not in fact the first to compose in lyric metres, as Catullus had composed poems (11 and 51) in the Sapphic metre and Laevius had experimented with lyric metres in his (lost) *Erotopaegnia*. On the evidence available, however, Horace's achievement dwarfed that of his predecessors and so justifies his boast here. What is interesting is that few poets sought to surpass Horace's achievements in the centuries after his death and the *Odes* stands as a more or less solitary towering achievement.

The philosophical background

The *Odes* make good use of the ideas of more than one major philosophical school and it is worth describing here something of the flavour of the schools of the Stoics, the Cynics and the Epicureans.

The Stoics (founded by Zeno of Citium (335–263 BC)) preached a philosophy whereby only virtue leads to happiness, only the wise can be virtuous and so only the virtuous man is wise. Virtue/duty alone matters and we should beware of letting our passions or emotions distract us from what reason tells us is the correct way to live, even when the 'emotion' in question is understandable terror at imminent danger of torture and painful death as in the case of Regulus in *Odes* III.5. Virtue is shown in the ability to forgo selfish pleasures in the interest of the community and there were eminent Stoics who committed suicide as a model for the free man's final freedom to practise virtue – such as Cato when the victory of the dictator Caesar at Thapsus in April 46 BC told him that his free republic was now dead (see OCD s.v. 'Porcius Cato' (2)). The model for the Stoic sense of public duty was the hero Hercules (cf. *Odes* III.3.9 where Hercules is linked with Augustus (cf. also III.14.1)) and this underlies much of the ethics of the 'Roman Odes'

Over against this high-minded elevation of duty over inclination are the schools of the Cynics and the Epicureans. The Cynics were founded by Diogenes (412–321 BC) who famously scorned the trappings of society and culture and lived in a barrel in the manner of a dog (*kynikos* in Greek means 'like a dog'), preaching that we are animals in clothes and can only be wise and happy when we live according to our animal natures. A more sophisticated version of cynicism is that of Epicurus (341–270 BC) who argued that we in fact seek pleasure and that goodness consists in what is likely to maximize pleasure over pain rather than the Stoic calculus of duty over inclination. The Epicureans did not, however, live a hedonistic lifestyle of orgies and banquets – they rather preached the wisdom of *parvum quod satis est* ('the little that is enough') and promoted an apolitical withdrawal from the world with the aim to 'live unnoticed' (cf. *Epistles* I.17.9–10). For them the ideal residence was a garden rather than the crowded Forum and (like the Cynics) they argued that we can only be happy when we fully accept the truth of the world which included the finality of death and the atomic nature of the universe. The advice to restrict our appetites and so be content with what is readily available is one which Horace repeats many times in his poetry (e.g. *Odes* III.16.37–44). The first of the 'Roman Odes' (III.1) is imbued with the Epicurean spirit of withdrawal into the simple life of the countryside and in his earlier poetry he had preached a very earthy Epicurean attitude towards sex (*Satires* I.2.114–19). Epicurus' attitude towards politics was very different from the *engagé* Stoics: on the one hand the wise Epicurean must avoid political ambition and the blind pursuit of power for the sake of a transient reputation: Lucretius demythologises the sinner Sisyphus – doomed to push a boulder up a hill for all eternity – as the symbol of the man driven by political ambition (III.995–1002: cf. also Lucretius III.59–64). On the other hand, the wise man will be quite content to live in a state ruled by a monarch who lets him get on with his philosophizing in peace: as Oscar Wilde is reputed to have said, the trouble with Socialism is that it takes up too many evenings.

Horace may have jokingly called himself 'a pig from the herd of Epicurus' (*Epistles* I.4.15–16) but he states that he did not 'sign up' to any of these schools – he described himself as *nullius addictus iurare in verba magistri* ('bound to swear allegiance to no master' *Epistles* I.1.14). That said, it is impossible to read Horace without meeting ideas and attitudes which can be traced back to those of the philosophical schools which provided much of the ethical thinking of the day.

The metre

Latin poetry is constructed in rhythmic patterns or 'metres' which are based on the length of syllables rather than verbal stress. Every vowel is either long or short by nature, although a short vowel is usually lengthened when it is followed by two or more consonants (so *immeritŭs* is scanned as *immeritūs* when the word *lues* follows it in VI.1). Double vowels (diphthongs, such as the first syllable of *Poenos*) are long by nature, as are some case-endings (e.g. ablative singular of the 1st declension, although the nominative singular -*a* ending is short).

The four poems in this book are all composed in the Alcaic metre, named after the Greek poet Alcaeus. The pattern is this, where

∪ = a short syllable

— = a long syllable

and 'x'= a syllable which may be either long or short: there is usually a word-break ('caesura', indicated by //) after the fifth syllable of the first two lines.

x — U — —// — UU — U x
x — U — —// — UU — U x
x — U — — — U — x
— UU — UU — U —x

aūdītĭs ān mē //lūdĭt ămābĭlĭs
īnsānĭ(a?) aūdīr(e)//ēt vĭdĕōr pĭōs
ērrārĕ pēr lūcōs, ămoēnaē
quōs ĕt ăquāe sŭbĕūnt ĕt aūraē.

Latin also had a word stress which fell on the penultimate syllable of a word (or the antepenultimate syllable if the penultimate was short). If one looks at the above stanza one hears the variety in how this word stress might have sounded.

aūdītĭs ān mē //lūdĭt ămābĭlĭs
īnsānĭ(a?) aūdīr(e)//ēt vĭdĕōr pĭōs
ērrārĕ pēr lūcōs, ămoēnaē
quōs ĕt ăquāe sŭbĕūnt ĕt aūraē.

Further reading

The literature on Horace is vast and this is a small selection of some books which students may find helpful in exploring the works of this poet.

Translations of the *Odes* include:

Rudd, N. (2004), *Odes and Epodes* (Loeb Classical Library), Cambridge, MA: Harvard: University Press,with facing Latin text.

West, D. (2008), *The Complete Odes and Epodes* (Oxford World's Classics), Oxford: Oxford University Press.

Editions of book 3 include:

Nisbet, R.G.M. and N. Rudd (2004), *A Commentary on Horace Odes Book III*, Oxford: Oxford University Press.

West, D. (2002), *Horace Odes III: Dulce Periculum*, Oxford: Oxford University Press.

Williams, G. (1969), *The Third Book of Horace's Odes*, Oxford: Oxford University Press.

General books on Horace:

Fraenkel, E. ([1957]2000), *Horace*, Oxford: Oxford University Press, new edn.

Harrison, S., ed (2007), *The Cambridge Companion to Horace*, Cambridge: Cambridge University Press.

Hills, P. (2005), *Horace*, London: Bloomsbury.

West, D. (1967), *Reading Horace*, Edinburgh: Edinburgh University Press.

On the *Odes* see especially:

Commager, S. (1995), *The Odes of Horace*, Norman, OK: University of Oklahoma Press, new edn.

Lowrie, M. (1997), *Horace's Narrative Odes*, Oxford: Oxford University Press.

Lowrie, M., ed (2009), *Horace: Odes and Epodes* (Oxford Readings in Classical Studies), Oxford: Oxford University Press.

On Horace and Augustus see:

Fowler, D.P. (2009), 'Horace and the Aesthetics of Politics', in M. Lowrie (ed), *Horace: Odes and Epodes* (Oxford Readings in Classical Studies), Oxford: Oxford University Press.

Griffin, J. (1984), 'Augustus and the Poets: "Caesar qui cogere posset"', in F. Millar and E. Segal (eds), *Caesar Augustus: Seven Aspects*, Oxford: Oxford University Press.

Lyne, R.O.A.M. (1995), *Horace – Behind the Public Poetry*, Yale: Yale University Press.

On the moral and social legislation see:

Edwards, C. (1993), *The Politics of Immorality in Ancient Rome*, Cambridge: Cambridge University Press, pp. 34–62.

On the use of metre see:

Morgan, L. (2010), *Musa Pedestris – Metre and Meaning in Roman Verse*, Oxford: Oxford University Press.

Raven, D.S. (2010), *Latin Metre*, Bloomsbury: London, new edn.

Useful books on Latin grammar used in this edition include:

Allen, J.H. and J.B. Greenough (2006), *New Latin Grammar*, New York: Dover Publications, referred to in the commentary as AG.

Morwood, J. (1999), *Latin Grammar*, Oxford: Oxford University Press.

For more information on all things ancient see:

The Oxford Classical Dictionary (OCD).

The best Latin dictionary available in English is:

The Oxford Latin Dictionary (OLD).

Text

2

angustam amice pauperiem pati
robustus acri militia puer
    condiscat et Parthos feroces
    vexet eques metuendus hasta

vitamque sub divo et trepidis agat   5
in rebus. illum ex moenibus hosticis
    matrona bellantis tyranni
    prospiciens et adulta virgo

suspiret, eheu, ne rudis agminum
sponsus lacessat regius asperum   10
    tactu leonem, quem cruenta
per medias rapit ira caedes.

dulce et decorum est pro patria mori:
mors et fugacem persequitur virum,
    nec parcit imbellis iuventae   15
    poplitibus timidove tergo.

Virtus repulsae nescia sordidae
intaminatis fulget honoribus,
    nec sumit aut ponit secures
    arbitrio popularis aurae.   20

Virtus, recludens immeritis mori
caelum, negata temptat iter via
    coetusque vulgares et udam
    spernit humum fugiente pinna.
est et fideli tuta silentio   25
merces: vetabo, qui Cereris sacrum
    vulgarit arcanae, sub isdem
    sit trabibus fragilemque mecum

solvat phaselon; saepe Diespiter
neglectus incesto addidit integrum: 30
    raro antecedentem scelestum
    deseruit pede Poena claudo.

3

iustum et tenacem propositi virum
non civium ardor prava iubentium,
    non vultus instantis tyranni
    mente quatit solida neque Auster,

dux inquieti turbidus Hadriae,   5
nec fulminantis magna manus Iovis:
    si fractus illabatur orbis,
    impavidum ferient ruinae.

hac arte Pollux et vagus Hercules
enisus arces attigit igneas,   10
    quos inter Augustus recumbens
    purpureo bibit ore nectar.

hac te merentem, Bacche pater, tuae
vexere tigres indocili iugum

collo trahentes; hac Quirinus   15
Martis equis Acheronta fugit,

gratum elocuta consiliantibus
Iunone divis: 'Ilion, Ilion
    fatalis incestusque iudex
    et mulier peregrina vertit   20

in pulverem, ex quo destituit deos
mercede pacta Laomedon, mihi
    castaeque damnatum Minervae
    cum populo et duce fraudulento.

iam nec Lacaenae splendet adulterae   25
famosus hospes nec Priami domus
    periura pugnaces Achivos
    Hectoreis opibus refringit,

nostrisque ductum seditionibus
bellum resedit. protinus et graves   30
    iras et invisum nepotem,
    Troica quem peperit sacerdos,

Marti redonabo; illum ego lucidas
inire sedes, ducere nectaris
    sucos et adscribi quietis   35
    ordinibus patiar deorum.

dum longus inter saeviat Ilion
Romamque pontus, qualibet exsules
    in parte regnanto beati;
    dum Priami Paridisque busto   40

insultet armentum et catulos ferae
celent inultae, stet Capitolium
    fulgens triumphatisque possit
    Roma ferox dare iura Medis.

horrenda late nomen in ultimas 45
extendat oras, qua medius liquor
    secernit Europen ab Afro,
    qua tumidus rigat arva Nilus,

aurum irrepertum et sic melius situm,
cum terra celat, spernere fortior 50
    quam cogere humanos in usus
    omne sacrum rapiente dextra.

quicumque mundo terminus obstitit,
hunc tanget armis, visere gestiens,
    qua parte debacchentur ignes, 55
    qua nebulae pluviique rores.

sed bellicosis fata Quiritibus
hac lege dico, ne nimium pii
    rebusque fidentes avitae
    tecta velint reparare Troiae. 60

Troiae renascens alite lugubri
fortuna tristi clade iterabitur,
    ducente victrices catervas
    coniuge me Iovis et sorore.

ter si resurgat murus aeneus 65
auctore Phoebo, ter pereat meis
    excisus Argivis, ter uxor
    capta virum puerosque ploret.'

non hoc iocosae conveniet lyrae:
quo, Musa, tendis? desine pervicax 70
    referre sermones deorum et
    magna modis tenuare parvis.

4

descende caelo et dic age tibia
regina longum Calliope melos,
    seu voce nunc mavis acuta
    seu fidibus citharave Phoebi.

auditis an me ludit amabilis   5
insania? audire et videor pios
    errare per lucos, amoenae
    quos et aquae subeunt et aurae.

me fabulosae Vulture in Apulo
nutricis extra limen Apuliae   10
    ludo fatigatumque somno
    fronde nova puerum palumbes

texere, mirum quod foret omnibus,
quicumque celsae nidum Acherontiae
    saltusque Bantinos et arvum   15
    pingue tenent humilis Forenti,

ut tuto ab atris corpore viperis
dormirem et ursis, ut premerer sacra
    lauroque collataque myrto,
    non sine dis animosus infans.   20

vester, Camenae, vester in arduos
tollor Sabinos, seu mihi frigidum
    Praeneste seu Tibur supinum
    seu liquidae placuere Baiae.

vestris amicum fontibus et choris   25
non me Philippis versa acies retro,

devota non exstinxit arbos
nec Sicula Palinurus unda.

utcumque mecum vos eritis, libens
insanientem navita Bosphorum   30
    temptabo et urentes harenas
    litoris Assyrii viator,

visam Britannos hospitibus feros
et laetum equino sanguine Concanum,
    visam pharetratos Gelonos   35
    et Scythicum inviolatus amnem.

vos Caesarem altum, militia simul
fessas cohortes abdidit oppidis,
    finire quaerentem labores
    Pierio recreatis antro.   40

vos lene consilium et datis et dato
gaudetis, almae. scimus ut impios
    Titanas immanemque turbam
    fulmine sustulerit caduco,

qui terram inertem, qui mare temperat   45
ventosum, et urbes regnaque tristia
    divosque mortalesque turmas
    imperio regit unus aequo.

magnum illa terrorem intulerat Iovi
fidens iuventus horrida bracchiis   50
    fratresque tendentes opaco
    Pelion imposuisse Olympo.

sed quid Typhoeus et validus Mimas,
aut quid minaci Porphyrion statu,
    quid Rhoetus evulsisque truncis   55
      Enceladus iaculator audax

contra sonantem Palladis aegida
possent ruentes? hinc avidus stetit
    Vulcanus, hinc matrona Iuno et
      numquam umeris positurus arcum,   60

qui rore puro Castaliae lavit
crines solutos, qui Lyciae tenet
    dumeta natalemque silvam,
      Delius et Patareus Apollo.

vis consili expers mole ruit sua: 65
vim temperatam di quoque provehunt
    in maius; idem odere vires
      omne nefas animo moventes.

testis mearum centimanus Gyas
sententiarum, notus et integrae   70
    temptator Orion Dianae,
      virginea domitus sagitta.

iniecta monstris Terra dolet suis
maeretque partus fulmine luridum
    missos ad Orcum; nec peredit   75
      impositam celer ignis Aetnen,

incontinentis nec Tityi iecur
reliquit ales, nequitiae additus
    custos; amatorem trecentae
      Perithoum cohibent catenae.   80

6

delicta maiorum immeritus lues,
Romane, donec templa refeceris
    aedesque labentes deorum et
      foeda nigro simulacra fumo.

dis te minorem quod geris, imperas: 5
hinc omne principium, huc refer exitum:
    di multa neglecti dederunt
      Hesperiae mala luctuosae.

iam bis Monaeses et Pacori manus
non auspicatos contudit impetus   10
    nostros et adiecisse praedam
      torquibus exiguis renidet.

paene occupatam seditionibus
delevit urbem Dacus et Aethiops,
    hic classe formidatus, ille   15
      missilibus melior sagittis.

fecunda culpae saecula nuptias
primum inquinavere et genus et domos;
    hoc fonte derivata clades
      in patriam populumque fluxit.   20

motus doceri gaudet Ionicos
matura virgo et fingitur artibus,
    iam nunc et incestos amores
      de tenero meditatur ungui;

mox iuniores quaerit adulteros 25
inter mariti vina, neque eligit
 cui donet impermissa raptim
 gaudia luminibus remotis,

sed iussa coram non sine conscio
surgit marito, seu vocat institor 30
 seu navis Hispanae magister,
 dedecorum pretiosus emptor.

non his iuventus orta parentibus
infecit aequor sanguine Punico,
 Pyrrhumque et ingentem cecidit 35
 Antiochum Hannibalemque dirum;

sed rusticorum mascula militum
proles, Sabellis docta ligonibus
 versare glebas et severae
 matris ad arbitrium recisos 40

portare fustes, sol ubi montium
mutaret umbras et iuga demeret
 bobus fatigatis, amicum
 tempus agens abeunte curru.

damnosa quid non imminuit dies? 45
aetas parentum peior avis tulit
 nos nequiores, mox daturos
 progeniem vitiosiorem.

Commentary

2

This poem is about the qualities which are desirable in a good (Roman) man, in particular one who contributes to public life. The poem is written in the historical and cultural context of Augustan Rome, an age which both praised the blessings of peace and also celebrated the virtues of military might and courage. The civil wars had been a period of anger directed against Roman citizens (amongst others): the new regime celebrated the ending of warfare with the symbolic closing of the gates of the temple of Janus in 25 BC, but there was still scope for the righteous quest to bring back the standards lost to the Parthians in 53 BC, a campaign which was not to find fulfilment until after the publication of the *Odes* but which was anticipated from 27 BC onwards.

The first poem in *Odes* book III was one in which the poet professed to scorn the pursuit of wealth and power and ended with him happy to stay on his humble farm rather than to seek wealth. Ode II starts with the image of the young Roman soldier, a *puer* such as Horace has been addressing since the previous ode (III.1.4). The figure of the boy is filled out here with more details of the qualities he is to develop, from hardy toughness to military ferocity, all controlled by a moral and religious modesty such as we see described again in VI.37–44. The second half of the poem then broadens the concept of *virtus* into more political and social qualities which avoid the snakepit of political ambition and which seek immortality through good behaviour. The poem ends with a sharp warning against the perils of indiscretion and the certainty of retribution for wrongdoing.

1 The poet picks up the theme of poverty from the end of the previous ode with the promoted word **angustam** ('straitened', 'narrow') applied to **pauperiem. amice** is an adverb, meaning 'like a friend'; making a friend of something which most people would shun is surprising and is the first of several paradoxes in this poem. Poverty (or at least a hardy austerity) is something which some (wealthy) Romans romanticized either positively or simply in antipathy towards luxury (see Juvenal 12 for both simultaneously). The ability to be happy on restricted means is something Horace espouses frequently; he ended the previous ode (III.1.48) asking why he should swap his humble Sabine estate for 'riches which bring more toil', having depicted the sorrows of the anxious rich man in 34–40: cf. II.18.1–2.

2 This boy is 'sturdy' (**robustus**). The key phrase **acri militia** is sandwiched between **robustus** and **puer**: suggesting that his toughness will be the result of the 'harsh military service'.

3–4 The two lines each begin with a strong verb in the present jussive subjunctive ('let him learn … let him harass'). The boy will need to 'learn' to endure poverty as such virtue is not inborn, but by the time we get to line 4 he is already able to use a spear and a horse in combat against the 'fierce Parthians'. **metuendus** is a gerundive describing the boy as 'one to be feared'.

5 sub divo means 'under the open sky'. *sub caelo* would have fitted the metre equally well and the word *divus* clearly denotes Jupiter, the Indo-European sky-god and the master of all as described in IV.45–8. The boy lives under the shelter and the fear of the gods, his hardy lifestyle having thus theological as well as practical associations and the placing of **trepidis** within the line also giving him a sense of appropriate fear. The line is neatly framed by the main verb (**vitam … agat**).

6–10 The poet passes from the masculine virtue of the boy himself to the effects this has on women. One might expect that the mother-figure here would be the boy's own mother nervous of his going out to fight the ferocious enemy, but in fact it is the mother of the enemy king. She is like Hecuba, mother of Hector, gazing out from the walls of the city of Troy (**ex moenibus hosticis**) at this Achilles who is going to kill her son, and the scene is an amalgamation of two scenes from Homer's *Iliad*: Helen looking from the walls of Troy at III.161–244 and Andromache seeing her husband Hector being dragged at XXII.463–5. Horace brings in a romantic touch such as we find when the crazy girl Scylla falls in love with her father's enemy Minos as she sees him attacking the city (Ovid *Metamorphoses* VIII.11–37).

8 The 'grown virgin' is the enemy prince's fiancée (he is her **sponsus**: see line 10) and she fears for her bridegroom's life.

9 eheu is an exclamation of regret or sorrow ('alas!') and is here the cry which the poet imagines being uttered by the **adulta virgo**, stressing this by placing the word immediately after the key verb **suspiret**. The verb is again in the jussive subjunctive, showing that this is what the poet wishes to happen ('let her sigh alas') followed by the fear-clause (**ne**) explaining her anxieties.

9–11 There is a strong contrast between the enemy who is new to the business of fighting (**rudis agminum**; words denoting experience (or lack of it) often take a defining term in the genitive) and the Roman youth who is a 'lion rough to the touch', a contrast familiar from epic where often the victim is an innocent lamb facing a savage lion/bull (e.g. Homer *Iliad* XXII.308–10). The verb **lacessat** suggests unnecessary provocation and nicely conveys both the naïve youth's bravado and the girl's panic. **Sponsus … regius** is the girl's view of her man: he is of royal blood and he is her fiancé – both good reasons to fear for his life and to expect him to be a target. **asperum tactu** means literally 'rough in the touching', with *tactu* the ablative form of the supine form of the verb *tango*. The form is common in epic poetry (e.g. *miserabile visu* Virgil *Aeneid* I.111).

11–12 The imagery here is strong. The youth has 'bloody anger' which is 'anger which will shed blood' and it 'carries him along' (**rapit**) through the middle of the slaughter – no backing off from the conflict for him. The imagery would of course apply perfectly to a lion, and the comparison of the warrior with a lion is as old as Homer (*Iliad* X.485–6, etc.).

13 One of the most famous lines in all literature, familiar to modern readers above all from Wilfred Owen's poem *Dulce et decorum est*, and another startling paradox. Dying for one's fatherland is of course honourable (**decorum**) as had been sung by war poets before (e.g. the early Spartan poet Tyrtaeus X.1–2) but the poet also tells us that it is 'sweet'. This is going too far for many people who would reply that the poet is romanticizing the grim reality of bloodshed.

14 The idealism of line 13 is undercut and qualified by the realism of 14, enhanced by the picking up of **mori** from the end of 13 with the noun **mors** at the beginning of this line. The choice is not between death and life but (it seems) between glorious death and a coward's death, which makes the 'sweetness' of death in 13 more believable if only in relative terms. Note here also the way in which the heroic death is despatched in one line (13) while the coward's death is dramatized with grim details over three lines.

14–16 The coward may be a man (**virum**) or a youth (**iuventae**) with no taste for war (**imbellis**) but death will still chase after him, even (**et**) if he flees. The coward is running away (**fugacem**) and so it is natural that his wounds will be on the back of his body: note here the personification of the man's back as itself **timido** and the grisly detail of the 'hamstrings' (**poplitibus**). It was standard practice in ancient warfare to disable one's fleeing opponents by slitting the hamstrings on the backs of their legs.

17 The scene changes suddenly from the more obvious theatre of manliness which is warfare to the murkier world of politics and social behaviour. **virtus** means 'that which distinguishes a (real) *vir*' and here has more of the sense of fearless integrity than merely courage in the face of physical danger. It is noteworthy that this and the following stanza both begin with this key word **virtus** as the poet seeks to refine his definition of the term.

17–20 This is a transitional stanza in the argument of the poem. Anyone who involves himself in politics will probably end up suffering defeat at the polls (**repulsae**) and the only way to avoid this is to avoid standing in the first place. Epicureans famously believed that political ambition is a labour of Sisyphus and that the wise man will live in philosophical obscurity (cf. Lucretius III.59–64) and so it looks as if Horace is here turning apolitical in revulsion at the corruption of late republican Roman politics where the likes of a Clodius could subvert the idealism of a Cicero or a Cato. This is enhanced by the use of words like **honoribus** here which usually applies to political distinction (cf. *Odes* I.1.8) and above all **secures** which were (along with the *fasces*) the symbols of consular office. In the Roman republic such offices were secured by catching (or buying) votes ('at the whim of the popular breeze') and the new Roman (and the new Roman emperor Augustus) does not need this sort of political success to demonstrate his **virtus**.

17–18 The imagery is that of the clean and the dirty: **sordidae** denotes 'filthy' and is contrasted with the 'unsullied' (**intaminatis** – a word only found here in classical Latin) honours, with the notion of 'bright and clean' brought out in the verb **fulget** ('shines'). The metaphor of 'shining with honours' (in the instrumental ablative) is nicely put.

19–20 The fickleness and changeability of the breeze makes it an excellent metaphor for the changing favours of the *mobile vulgus* (whence our English word 'mob'). **arbitrio** means 'at the decision' and again brings out the paradox whereby these axes which represented the physical power of the consul over the people were now being given or withheld by the whim of the people.

21 *recludo* comes from *re-claudo* and so means 'unlock'. In the opening lines of the poem we heard about the brave youth who faces death nobly – here we meet those who 'do not deserve to die', whose courage and excellence have granted them immortality. Such men include Hercules (who died on the pyre on Mt Oeta but was raised to immortality in recognition of his labours and married to the goddess Hebe). That such is not the common lot of humanity is brought home with the term **negata via** ('on a path denied [to ordinary men]') in line 22.

22 There is effective juxtaposition of **iter via** here which helps to set up the theme of swift flight from the earth in the following lines.

23 virtus shuns the 'vulgar gatherings': this (to us) snobbish and contemptuous term reminds us of the opening of the first ode in this book (*odi profanum vulgus et arceo* ('I hate the unholy crowd and shun them')) which itself recalls the stance of the influential Greek poet Callimachus (*Epigram* XXX.4: 'I hate all things of the people').

23–4 The imagery is that of Stoicism (itself drawing on Platonism before it) whereby the four elements are divided into heavy ones (earth and water) and light ones (fire and air): fire and air coalesce into the fine air known as 'aether' which surrounds the earth and to which our souls fly on death; see also *Satires* II.2.79.

25-6 The virtue of discretion is singled out as an additional (**et**) good quality: keeping silence when it would be a breach of trust not to do so (hence the stress on **fideli**). Horace may be alluding to the need for an imperial confidante to keep his emperor's confidences secret – something which Augustus certainly cared about.

26-9 Horace neatly sidesteps the political resonance of 'faithful silence' with a reference to the famously secretive rites of Ceres, the Eleusinian Mysteries. The poet now switches from the third person to the first person (**vetabo ... mecum**) in a personal tone which is characteristic of lyric poetry. The Latin requires us to take **arcanae** with **Cereris** (the rites of secret Ceres) in hypallage for 'the secret rites of Ceres'. **vulgarit** reminds us of **vulgares** in 23 and is a contracted form of *vulgaverit* (future perfect of *vulgo*). The construction after **vetabo** is slightly complex: we have to understand '*illum*' (or some such) to be picked up by qui, and then the subjunctives **sit** and **solvat** are dependent on *vetabo* in the sense 'I shall forbid him to be' (literally, 'that he be ... that he cast off').

There were those who feared that the gods would punish miscreants with disaster and that the innocent bystander would be killed along with the guilty (cf. VI.5), hence the blanket ban (**vetabo**) on anyone like this from being 'under the same beams' or 'untying the delicate boat' with him. The choice of words is deliberate and effective: the roof overhead consists of wooden beams which could fall down, and the boat is only a small one (**phaselon**: cf. Catullus 4) and is **fragilem** (easily broken up).

29 Diespiter is the archaic form of the name *Jupiter* and here has the effect of making the poet sound solemn and piously old-fashioned – as befits the *Musarum sacerdos* of *Odes* III.1.2.

30 The nature of the offence to the god has changed: in lines 25–9 it was the revelation of divine secrets, whereas here it is the refusal to pay due honour to the god, a 'neglect' which the god will soon rectify by bringing himself unpleasantly to their attention, as the poet warns again at VI.7–8. The line has an incantatory effect with the assonance of 'e' (**neglectus incesto**) and then 'i' (**add*i*d*i*t *i*nteg-**) and there is also a priest-like certainty about the statement emphasized by **saepe** (29) which is suggestive of wise experience.

31–2 The poem ends with a personified image of Punishment (**Poena**) chasing with a limping foot (**pede ... claudo**) after the sinner. The statement is made in a negative rather than positive form, with **raro** showing a similar claim to priestly knowledge as we saw with **saepe** in **29**. The sinner has put a great distance between himself and retribution, a distance brought out by the lengthy phrasing and the long word **antecedentem** – but she does not give up often and the tap-tap of her (lame) footsteps is echoed in the alliteration of **pede Poena. deseruit** is a gnomic perfect – that is, a perfect tense used to express a generalized statement ('Punishment rarely gives up on the chase'). **pede ... claudo** is an ablative of description ('Punishment with her limping foot').

3

The previous ode discussed the route to immortality through virtue (III.2.21–4) and ended with the just man avoiding the punishment which confronts the wicked. This poem begins with a similar image of the just man achieving immortality and includes Augustus as one such. The bulk of the poem (XVIII–68) is a long speech by the goddess Juno warning of the dire consequences if the Romans seek to rebuild the ruined city of Troy. Crucial to the unity of the poem is the figure of Romulus, allowed to be deified by Juno (XXXI–6) for all her hostility to him (31): the glorious future of Romulus' descendants is nicely pitched against the humiliating ruins of Troy itself, and this ties in with both the theme of deification of great men (such as Augustus) and the use made of Romulus by the regime as a focus for patriotic fervour (there was even the suggestion that Augustus might adopt the name Romulus at one point in his early years as emperor). As in the previous poem, there is the warning of the need to exercise caution and imperial restraint – only for the poet to finish his ode with a call to exercise literary restraint and to avoid aspiring to such grand themes.

The content of Juno's speech raises some questions. Did anyone actually want to rebuild Troy? Or was this just a poetical conceit on the part of Horace? West argues that the poet is thanking Augustus for resisting Antony's desire to move the centre of power from Rome to Alexandria – but Egypt is not Troy and it is hard to prove such a tenuous link here. It is perhaps more likely that Horace is alluding to the legend whereby the anger of Juno, which his fellow-poet Virgil was analysing in his *Aeneid* (composed in the 20s BC), was finally laid to rest on the strict explicit condition that the new race formed by the union of Aeneas and the natives of Latium would speak Italian and not Trojan and that Troy itself would remain destroyed for ever (as enunciated explicitly in Juno's speech in Virgil *Aeneid* XII.818–28). What we have here then is Horace mimicking the epic themes of the *Aeneid* and stealing some of the language of the epic in his lyric evocation of the values which he espoused in his role as *Musarum sacerdos*. The lyric form is not suited to an epic narrative and so the poet conveys the historical themes through the medium of an impassioned speech drawing on both Homer and Ennius, whose first book of *Annales* contained a 'council of the gods' to discuss the deification of Romulus. Similarly, the following two odes will show a mixture of literary models, as III.4 uses material drawn from Hesiod and III.5 will use material from historical sources to dramatize the heroic acts of Regulus.

This would, however, reduce the poem to a literary pastiche and it is hard to imagine Horace putting this sort of poem in this position in the Roman Odes. Troy was regarded as something of a byword for luxury and even debauchery and the theme of sexual immorality which will be so prominent in poem 6 is here adumbrated with the figures of the *incestus iudex* Paris and the *Lacaenae adulterae* whom he abducted. The upshot of all this is that this poem is probably the most enigmatic of those in this volume, and that what appear to be clear categories (Troy – Romulus – Augustus – virtue) resist easy interpretation.

The chronology of the speech is interesting: the speech of Juno supporting the deification of Romulus has to take place some years after the end of the Trojan War and yet Juno still smarts from the hurt caused her before that war had even begun. Gods are good haters: and Virgil had also raised the question *tantaene animis caelestibus irae?* ('Do divine souls have such great causes of wrath?') in *Aeneid* I.11. Furthermore, the speech of Juno is long past by the time of Horace and the reader is left with the question of whether the Romans of his day have met the terms of Juno's ancient prophecy.

1–6 The poem opens with a long and grandiose statement of the just man's resistance to outside forces, with the accusative object (**iustum ... virum**) followed by four separate subject phrases (**ardor ... vultus ... Auster ... manus**).

1 The poem begins emphatically with the key word **iustum**; and the phrase **iustum ... virum** frames the line, with **virum** picking up the theme of *virtus* (i.e. *vir-tus*) from the previous poem. *tenax* derives from *teneo* and the term means 'keeping hold of', taking (as here) a genitive of the thing being held. **propositi** may seem somewhat vague ('that which has been set up by him' and so 'purpose' – whatever that may be) but if the man is truly just then his 'purpose' will also be righteous and the two-word phrase **tenacem propositi** almost becomes a single concept ('determined'). The Stoic ideal of *virtus* demanded this sort of ability to withstand pressures both from the outside (society) and also from within (our own passions).

2–3 Political pressure is seen from below (the 'blazing' passion of the citizens 'ordering' what is crooked) and then in line 3 from above (the 'tyrant'); both are ineffectual in shaking the man of integrity. The language is very well chosen: the mob is here on fire with passion and their orders are for 'crooked things' (**prava** – neuter plural as object of **iubentium**), with the passion and the crookedness in effective juxtaposition. In poem 2 (30) the mob was regarded as a fickle breeze blowing (*arbitrio popularis aurae*). Then we only see the 'face' of the tyrant who is 'lowering' over him. The exercise of authority is not in itself a bad thing and Horace is careful to use the foreign term **tyranni** for the autocrat whose power is not inherited or legitimate. Augustus was of course not a 'tyrant' but rather merely *princeps*, although some Romans might have thought *tyrannus* also fitted his regime.

4–5 The enjambement over the first two stanzas is expressive of the wind sweeping over the sea: and the wind is yet another 'leader' (**dux**) whose authority the wise man will not bow before. Here the wind is described in almost political terms – **turbidus** suggests *turba* ('crowd') with the sense of 'rabble-rousing' or 'rebellious', and **inquieti** is a reminder of the passionate mob with their orders in the first stanza. There is a neat surprise here also in that the wind is master of the Adriatic but for all that he is powerless to shake this man.

6 Horace is not saying that the virtuous man will not fear the gods but rather the lightning blast which was seen as expressing the power of the sky-god. There is a touch of anthropomorphism in the lightning seen in personal terms as being thrown by 'the great hand of thundering Jupiter' the sky-god.

7–8 The opening passage closes with a neat hyperbolic summary. Even if the whole firmament is shattered (**fractus**) and were to crash down (**illabatur** is a hypothetical subjunctive in a conditional) then the just man will not be afraid although the debris will strike him: **ferient** is a strong future indicative showing the certainty of the wise man's fate and (by implication) the certainty of his attitude. Strength consists in facing down threats, not in minimizing them, and the cosmic threat successfully closes the list which has moved from the very real (politics and sea-storms) to the less probable (thunderbolts) and now to the total destruction of the world around him. If he can face this, he really can face anything.

9 hac arte ('by this virtue') denotes the fixity of purpose presented in lines 1–8. **Pollux** was one of the twin sons of Jupiter (along with his brother Castor) while **Hercules** (also a child of Jupiter) was the hero famed for his twelve labours which rid the world of many threatening monsters and made human life more bearable. Hercules was something of a Stoic role-model – cf. Virgil *Aeneid* VIII.185–279 – who had to travel far and wide to perform his labours – hence the description here of him as **vagus**.

10 For the Stoic imagery of the 'fiery citadels' see the note on II.23–4: the vision of the divine abode begins as more Stoic than Homeric, but this is going to change with the next two lines where the poet startles us with a very anthropomorphic vision of the divine banquet with a very recognizable special guest.

11–12 Horace uses the emperor's honorific name (**Augustus** was not his civil name (which was Gaius Julius Caesar Octavianus) but more of a title meaning 'worthy of reverence' conferred on him in 27 BC. See the Introduction for more details on Augustus' rise to power). So here it makes sense for a man with such venerable qualities to be sitting amongst the blessed gods. The imagery is of a divine banquet: Augustus is reclining as Romans did at dinner and he is drinking the nectar which the gods drank. The text printed here reads the present tense **bibit** which seems on the face of it unlikely – how could a living emperor be already drinking with the gods? Many texts print the future tense *bibet* which makes more obvious sense and points to the hope that he would be deified one day (as his adoptive father Julius Caesar had been). The reading printed can be justified as forming part of the poetic vision which exists in 'real time' for the poet; this has the added effect of making the vision of a divine Augustus less 'real' and more obviously a poetic fantasy. For this idea of the apotheosis of the emperor see Virgil *Aeneid* I.289–90 and for a satirical take on the business see Seneca's *Apocolocyntosis* ('Pumpkinification') of the recently deceased emperor Claudius. The deification of the emperor is elsewhere in the Roman Odes (III.5.2–4) regarded as linked to (but not necessarily conditional on) his conquering of Britain and Parthia.

purpureo denotes the deep red which was (presumably) the colour of the wine-like nectar which stains the drinker's lips: the word is also a byword for lavish luxury and royal splendour and so befits the imperial/divine context.

13–15 The construction is: 'by this [virtue], O father Bacchus, your tigers took you deservedly (**merentem**), dragging the yoke with a neck which cannot be tamed.' Bacchus deserved the elevation to divinity because he gave mankind the gift of the vine, and his chariot was often (e.g. Virgil *Aeneid* VI.805) described as being drawn by tigers. Notice the anaphora of **hac … hac …** which nicely joins together lines 9–18, giving a more smooth transition from the opening generalization to the mythical material of Romulus and Juno.

15–16 Quirinus was the formal name for the deified Romulus, which is highly significant in this poem. Romulus was the founder of Rome and the child of the god Mars and the priestess Rhea Silvia.

Rhea claimed descent from Troy: her father Numitor belonged to royal family of Alba Longa which traced its ancestry back to Aeneas the Trojan, and in Ennius' account of the legend Ilia was Aeneas' daughter. Here the divine ancestry of Romulus is heightened by the juxtaposition over the line-break with **Martis**; and the speed of his deification is brought out by the reference to the 'horses' (i.e. the chariot) of Mars and the appropriate verb **fugit** (he 'fled'), recalling the *fugiente penna* in II.21–4.

17–18 The poem proposes that Romulus could not be deified until and unless his grandmother Juno gave her consent; and most of the rest of this poem is what purports to be her speech agreeing to what the other gods clearly wanted all along (**gratum**).

18–24 Ilion (here in the Greek form of the accusative case) was Troy and the passionate repetition of the name well evokes the strong feelings of the goddess. This is also shown by her repeated refusal to name the guilty pair in lines 19–20 and 25–6. The first seven lines of Juno's speech form one long sentence beginning with an exclamatory statement (**Ilion**) of the object of the verb followed by a pair of subjects (**iudex et mulier**) with a singular verb **vertit**, followed by a temporal clause (**ex quo**) and then rounded off with a new statement about the place with which the sentence began. The passion of the speaker is well evoked in the slightly jumbled syntax of the sentence.

19 The 'unchaste judge' was Paris, a Trojan asked by Jupiter to judge which of three goddesses (Venus, Juno and Minerva) was the most beautiful after a golden apple bearing the dedication 'to the most beautiful one' had been thrown by the goddess Eris ('Discord') into the wedding feast of Peleus and Thetis. Paris earns the description **incestus** because his prize for giving the apple to Venus (goddess of sexual love) was to have the very beautiful wife of the king of Sparta, Helen, who is here indignantly described as a 'foreign woman' (**mulier peregrina**). **fatalis** (to be taken with **iudex**) is emphasized by its position at the start of the line and suggests that the actions of this 'judge' were responsible for the doom of his city. There is also political resonance here in that Antony had made a bad judgement in choosing a 'foreign woman' (Cleopatra) over his wife Octavia (who was Augustus' sister). Horace's use of allusive terms to refer to Paris and Helen is good for expressing Juno's contempt for them but also leaves open the wider applications which readers could tap into.

21–23 ex quo means *ex quo tempore* ('from the time when') and is to be taken with **damnatum** (agreeing with the neuter name **Ilion** in line 18): the city was 'condemned ever since Laomedon'. Juno has no qualms about naming Laomedon, the father of Priam who cheated the gods Apollo and Neptune of the agreed fee for their help in building the walls of Troy. **destituit** means here 'cheated' or 'left [the gods] without' his 'pledged payment' (**mercede pacta**). Homer (*Iliad* V.638–42) tells us that Laomedon tried a similar trick on Hercules and was killed by him for it – all this is to bring out that Juno is motivated by the principle of divine superiority as well as the personal insult to her beauty which was the judgement of Paris. It is not immediately obvious why the trick played on two male gods should cause the trickster's city to be condemned by two female gods who had no direct role in the deal, and it is suspiciously coincidental that these two goddesses were the ones slighted by that other Trojan, Paris. There is a pattern here, however, in which Juno builds her case against Troy as a city of liars (cf. **fraudulento** (24) and **periura** (27)).

22-3 The dative cases of **mihi** and **Minervae** are datives of agent ('condemned by me and Minerva') and the final two lines of the sentence serve to bring out attention back to **Ilion**, its fate (**damnatum**) and the original reason for it in the telling final word **fraudulento** (24).

25–6 There is obvious gloating in the phrase **iam nec** ('not any more') and her hatred of Paris and Helen shows in her repeated refusal to name either of them; the terms also indicate the reason for their condemnation in that Paris (the 'infamous house-guest') abused the rights of a guest by seducing the wife of the host, and Helen ('the Spartan adulteress') was unfaithful to her husband. **splendet** is a good word for the 'preening' brilliance of Paris, and it is possible that **Lacaenae … adulterae** are in the dative case (rather than the genitive) as the person to whom Paris no longer 'shines'. For Helen's disillusion with her new husband see Homer *Iliad* III.428–36, although the point here in Juno's speech is that Paris is dead, rather than unappealing to Helen. The censorious tone of the word **adulterae** is a signal of the importance of sexual morality within marriage as part of the regime within which Augustus was seeking to impose moral legislation on the Roman people – legislation which would (in 18 BC) make adultery a capital offence and which would result in the banishment of the emperor's own daughter Julia; the theme is explored further in Ode VI.

26–7 There is obvious alliteration of 'p' here as Juno spits out her feelings.

28 Hector was the greatest warrior of the sons of Priam, being killed by Achilles in revenge for Hector's killing of Achilles' great friend Patroclus. Juno implies that the Trojans only managed to drive back the Greeks when Hector's 'help' (**opibus**) was available, and the sneer at their treachery in **periura** (27) repeats her feeling that they deserved to lose.

29–30 Was the war 'drawn out by (divine) quarrels'? Certainly there were disagreements amongst the gods who took sides – Apollo and Aphrodite/Venus, for instance, favouring Troy while Juno and Athena/Minerva favoured the Greeks. Juno suggests that their bickering prolonged the war and promotes her pose as the bringer of peace and stability. Note the assonant play on words in **seditionibus … resedit**.

30-1 The vindictive anger of Juno was of great ferocity – shown for instance in her ruining of Heracles in Euripides' *Heracles*, and seen as a prime motive force behind much of the action in Virgil's *Aeneid* (e.g. I.8–11). Here her decision to forgo her wrath is taken 'from now on' (**protinus**) with the same energy as the anger itself.

31-2 Mars was in some accounts Juno's son (see Hesiod *Theogony* 922-3) and so Romulus would then be her grandson. The child is **invisum** ('hated') because his mother Ilia/Rhea Silvia claimed descent from the hated Trojans (**Troica**): Ilia/Rhea Silvia was also a Vestal Virgin (hence **sacerdos**) who should not have borne children at all.

33 Marti redonabo is a compressed expression. The verb is an archaic one and means to 'renounce something' or to 'give up my resentment at'. It is to be taken both with **iras** ('I will renounce my anger') and then again with **nepotem** ('I will renounce any grudge against my hated grandson'). There is also a nice ambiguity as **Marti** follows straight on from the previous line and so the sense seems to be 'whom the Trojan priestess bore to Mars', until we see the verb **redonabo**.

33-6 The abode of the gods is described as a place of light (**lucidas**), of feasting (**nectaris sucos**), of peace (**quietis**) and of order (**ordinibus**). This is in keeping with one traditional Greco-Roman idea of the tranquillity of Olympus as found in Homer *Odyssey* VI.42–6 (cf. Lucretius III.18–24), although the peaceful surroundings do nothing to prevent some barnstorming arguments between gods in Homer's *Iliad* (e.g. XXIV.32–76) and Ovid's *Metamorphoses,* and even Zeus/Jupiter can weep tears of blood over his dead son Sarpedon (Homer *Iliad* XVII. 458–61). Romulus is envisaged here as being allowed to enter, to have a drink, and to take his proper place amongst the gods.

34-5 ducere here means 'to drink up' (OLD s.v. 'ducere' 25b) and the emphasis on nectar recalls the imagery of Augustus' lips stained red with the same drink in line 12, thus adding to the important link between Augustus and Romulus which is a major element of this poem.

35–6 adscribi denotes being 'enrolled' in the appropriate class of citizens, and the plural word **ordinibus** is suggestive of the rows of senators such as were observed in the theatre; this is a very Roman view of Olympus.

36 patiar continues the theme that Juno is in charge of all.

37–44 Juno spells out the deal in the coming lines with her terms laid out with an orderly anaphora of **dum … dum**: Trojan exiles may rule anywhere in the world except Troy itself which must remain a barren landscape. **dum** here means 'on condition that' and this usage always takes the subjunctive as here (**saeviat … insultet … celent**).

37–8 The order for translation is: *dum longus pontus saeviat inter Ilion Romamque* and the word order is interesting, placing the two cities together (albeit enjambed) on the page but insisting that they be kept apart in real life, the whole phrase framed by the massive sea which is in fact expected to lie *between* the two places. A weaker writer might have inverted the order and had the names framing the sea.

38–9 regnanto is a third-person future imperative (AG §448–9; 'Let them rule') which has an archaic tone – Latin more commonly used the jussive subjunctive (*regnent*) for this purpose. Juno speaks as queen of the gods and her language is airily dismissive with the indifferent qualifier **qualibet … in parte** (wherever they like) and the tart description of these future rulers as always being 'exiles'.

40–1 Great men care about the fate of their tombs but Juno insists that these tombs will be for cattle to trample on (**insultet** has more than a touch of mockery and abuse) and to use as a place to hide their young. The two famous men (Priam and Paris, both focussed on earlier at lines 19 and 26) are placed in grand alliterative juxtaposition and the shocking condition **insultet armentum** is emphasized by the enjambement and its position at the head of the following stanza.

41–2 Paris was the son of King Priam, and it is ironically apt that the tombs should allow wild animals to protect their own 'sons' where this father and son are buried. **inultae** is well placed at the end of the phrase for further shock value: anyone treating the royal family like this would be punished, but these wild beasts are not.

41–4 The glory of Rome is evoked in the 'gleaming Capitol' which is to remain standing whereas the city of Troy has fallen into the dust (20–21). The Capitoline hill was the smallest of the hills of Rome but was the citadel and the religious centre and symbol of Rome's greatness, with a gilded (hence **fulgens**) temple dedicated to Jupiter Optimus Maximus, Juno and Minerva: it was where triumphal processions ended and where public officials made vows and sacrifices (see OCD s.v. 'Capitol'). Rome is **ferox** (rather like the **ferae** now living in Troy). Her new subjects (and the objects of her 'triumph' on whom she wishes to impose laws (**iura**)) are Medes, that is, Parthians. This brings the poem right up to Horace's own day and the poet (here as at III.5.1–4, I.22.2) looks forward to a day when Parthia will be conquered. Augustus was to do something of this in 20 BC when he succeeded in bringing back the Roman standards taken by the Parthians after the battle of Carrhae in 53 BC and Horace joined in approval of the 'victory' (see *Odes* VI.15.6–8, *Epistles* I.12.27–8, 18.56).

43–4 possit is concessive ('fierce Rome may have the power to …'). The phrase is framed by the object of Roman civilizing conquest (**triumphatis … Medis**) and the word order enhances the sense that the civilizing laws come after the military defeat.

45–52 This is one long sentence, broken up as follows: (a) let Rome extend her power (**horrenda … oras**) (b) into the Mediterranean and Egypt (**qua … Nilus**), (c) as a race which can resist the power of gold (**aurum … dextra**).

45–7 horrenda late is emphasized at the head of the line, the stanza and the sentence: **horrenda** is a gerundive meaning 'one to be dreaded', and continues the idea of Rome conquering the Medes. **ultimas … oras** signifies the furthest shores to the west (the sea dividing Europe from Africa is the straits of Gibraltar) and the east (Egypt).

48 The river Nile was 'swollen' in that it irrigated the fields with plentiful water and so ensured the abundant harvests for which Egypt was famous. The fields (**arva**) here are verbally submerged in the waters of the surrounding words **rigat … Nilus**.

49–52 The Roman will show greater strength of character if he rejects the allure of gold and leaves it safely buried in the earth (49–50) or else where it is now in temples (52). The construction of the sentence is thus: Rome will be **fortior** to reject the gold which is undiscovered, rather than (**quam**) to use it. The infinitives are dependent on the (comparative) adjective as in *Odes* I.37.26 (see AG §461 for other examples). The order for translation is: *fortior spernere aurum irrepertum (et sic … celat) quam cogere.*

Gold could be mined as in Spain and elsewhere (see OCD s.v. 'gold') or else it could be stolen from temples as was done by, for example, Verres in Sicily, according to Cicero (*Verrines* II.1.54).

51–2 omne sacrum presumably refers to the gold of 49 along with everything else which is used for the worship of the gods and so 'sacred'. There is a nice pointing of the blasphemy inherent in using the divine for 'human purposes', and the instrumental ablative **rapiente**

dextra ('with rapacious hand') adds a suitably pejorative touch to the end of the sentence.

53–4 'Whatever boundary has been set to the world – Rome will touch this in conquest.' The exaggeration of Juno's fantasy might strike the reader as absurd (although similar prophecies are made by Jupiter to the anxious mother Venus in Virgil *Aeneid* I.278–82) but her tone throughout the speech is above all concessive: Rome can go as far as it likes so long as it does not rebuild Troy (58–60).

54–6 Juno nicely captures the ancient fascination with seeing the distant wonders of the world: **gestiens** suggests a real compulsion and the extremes are well conveyed in the fires and the misty waters which will be no barrier to the Roman. *debacchari* is 'to rage madly to the point of exhaustion', like a worshipper of Bacchus, and so here nicely means 'to burn oneself out'; this is suited to fires but less so the misty vapours of 56, where **nebulae** means 'clouds', **pluvii** 'rainy' and **rores** 'dew', the three words juxtaposed into a powerful unity of wetness. Neither extreme will be a barrier for the Roman – or for Juno granting them leave to touch them. Line 55 refers to the furthest south, while 56 refers to the north, completing the circle began in 46–8.

57–60 The crucial condition (**lege**). The Romans are referred to as the 'warlike Quirites' which is something of an oxymoron as *Quirites* indicates citizens as civilians and was used as a term of reproach by Caesar (Suetonius *Julius Caesar* 70) to his insufficiently belligerent troops; the tone is one of disgust with the men of peace fancying a new adventure, their sentimental loyalty to the place (**pii**) and their over-confidence (**fidentes**) getting the better of them. The obvious sense of **nimium pii** is that the Roman will be too loyal to his distant ancestry and seek to rebuild his ancestral (**avitae**) home in Troy: there is (one might think) nothing wrong with being *pius*, but Juno puts strict limits on it. **rebusque fidentes** indicates that they will be sufficiently confident of their power and wealth to risk such a far-flung venture. Note how the key name **Troiae** is left to the very end of the sentence, the line and the stanza, only to be repeated at once at the start of the following line.

61–4 Juno continues the threatening tone with the strong future indicative **iterabitur**, the ominous 'bird of bad omen' (**alite lugubri**), the mention of her victorious troops and finally the listing of her divine titles and power.

61 *ales* literally means 'bird' and here means 'omen' as the Romans often used to predict the future by observing the flight of birds (se OCD s.v. 'auspicium') – a practice as old as Homer (*Iliad* XII.200–9). **lugubri** is predicative of the grief which the omen portends and the phrase **alite lugubri** is in the ablative of 'attendant circumstances'.

62 Note here the elliptical surprise in the word **fortuna** – the 'fortune' of Troy will turn out to be their ruin – and the choice of **fortuna** expresses the hopes of the people rebuilding the doomed city. **iterabitur** means that the fortune 'will be repeated' (by means of the **tristi clade**) and is only ominous when one recalls the fate of the former Troy.

63–4 Juno was the sister and wife of Jupiter (cf. Virgil *Aeneid* I.46–7). Her statement here shows that she has power both directly as a direct descendant of Saturn/Cronos (and leader of victorious troops) and also indirectly through the sky-god Jupiter whose bed she shares.

65–8 The three verbs are all subjunctive in a 'less vivid' conditional (see AG §516b) referring to future time ('if the wall should rise up three times it would be destroyed three times, the captured wife would weep three times'). Note the inexorable power of the anaphora of **ter**, an epic device used in Homer (e.g. *Iliad* XVI.702–3, where Patroclus attacks the walls of Troy three times, only to be beaten back by Apollo three times – a passage which Horace recalls here).

65–6 The walls of Troy were built with the aid of Phoebus Apollo and Neptune (see note on 21–2) and the phrase is concessive in tone here – even if the new wall were made of bronze and had Phoebus behind its construction, it would still fall.

67 excisus (from *ex-caedo*) is a strong word – 'hewed out of its foundations'. Juno lays claim to the Greeks as 'my own' – presumably the same as the **victrices catervas** of 63 – and the use of an instrumental ablative (when we expect an ablative of agent with *a*) is powerful.

67–8 The misery and anguish of war is eloquently summarized in six words here, focalizing the suffering through the tears (**ploret**) of a captured woman weeping for her husband and her boys who have presumably been put to death by the victorious troops, her sobbing anguish felt in the alliteration and *o-e-* assonance of **puerosque ploret**. It is interesting that Juno's great speech ends with this pathetic vignette of the pain and suffering attendant upon conquest, an image which recalls that of the Trojan women such as Andromache.

69–72 Horace ends the poem with a sharp rebuke to his Muse and a reminder to her and to us that such great themes as this are not suited to the 'slender' form of lyric. **iocosae** ('cheerful', 'playful') suggests that the normal themes for his Muse are those of parties, love and laughter and amounts to the poet telling his Muse to 'lighten up'. This form of closure is known as a 'breaking off formula' and is a form of irony where the mood is broken by the poet reminding us that this is a poem and amounts to what Lowrie (*Horace's Narrative Odes* p. 228) calls an 'after the fact *recusatio*' – that is, an ironic distancing of the poet from his work after he has written it, reminding the audience that they are witnessing a performance of a crafted work of art, while also looking to the next poem which will feature the Muses heavily. For other examples of this sort of ending see. II.1.37–40, Theocritus I.127, Pindar *Nemean* IX.54–5, *Olympian* VI.105, Catullus 51.13–16.

72 The line is neatly phrased with the antithetical terms **magna … parvis**. The infinitive **tenuare** is interesting – its primary meaning ('to make thinner') is apt in the sense that the poet is pruning the traditional hexameter of such epic material and producing a slimmed down lyric version with shorter lines, but it also suggests the adjective *tenuis* ('subtle', 'fine') – a literary quality prized by the poets of Horace's generation.

4

This is a **longum … melos** (2) indeed; it is the longest of all Horace's *Odes* and is a wonderfully varied and interesting composition. It blends Greek and Latin, the past and the present, the personal and the political, the temporal and the spiritual. Throughout the first half of the poem stand the Muses, the nine female gods who were said to inspire the arts; they are credited with inspiring the poet (1–8) and with having protected him both when he was a child (9–20) and later on as an adult (21–36). They are assumed (40) to be the ones to grant refreshment to a tired Augustus. At this point the poem moves into an extended account of the failure of the Giants in their attempt to overthrow Jupiter and the poet can draw moralizing conclusions about the proper use of force. So if the first half of the poem expresses devotion to the Muses, the second half demonstrates what these Muses can generate in terms of poetic inspiration, especially as they are the divine beings who 'know the past, present and future' (Hesiod *Theogony* 27–8) and so are the authorities for the poet's information.

It is tempting to treat the Battle of the Giants (the 'Gigantomachy') as allegorical. The 'violence devoid of wisdom' could refer to the poet's own times either in general terms as the forces of civil war which had wrecked Rome or more specifically as the forces of Antony and Cleopatra. This would equate the emperor with Jupiter and glorify his triumphs as the victory of wisdom over brute force. Augustus has (of course) not been in power for long, and the episode could also be seen as a warning to him to rule with wisdom as well as violence. He has the choice of being Jupiter or a Giant, rather as Aeneas has the choice of becoming a Hercules or a Cacus in Virgil *Aeneid* VIII. Similarly, it is tempting to see Pirithous the 'lover' as standing for Mark Antony or even for the poet himself – who is no stranger to love (III.26.1–2). Once again, the thought of the poem (65) is clear that love in itself is not a bad thing, but that when used without wisdom (and Pirithous tried to abduct Persephone by force) it will bring disaster, just like the violence of the Giants.

The lyrical treatment of the 'Gigantomachy' and the address to the lyre itself owe a lot to Pindar's first *Pythian* ode (quoted in Greek and in English in the accompanying web resources). Pindar's poem was composed to celebrate the victory (in the chariot race at the Pythian Games) of Hieron, who lived at Aetna in Sicily: the references to the volcanic mountain burying the mythical Giant Typhoeus are clearly more topical for Pindar here than they are for Horace, although Pindar does make use of the tale of Typhoeus even when the dedicatee is not Sicilian (e.g. *Pythian* VIII written for Aristomenes of Aigina). The influence of Pindar is also felt strongly in the autobiographical section of the poem where the infant poet is saved from animals by the Muses: Pindar recounts (*Olympian* VI. 45–7) being fed as a baby by two serpents with 'the blameless venom of the honeybee' and the late author Pausanias tells (IX.23.2) the tale of the young Pindar falling asleep on his walk to Thespiae and having wax laid on his lips by bees as an initiation into the life of a poet. Horace was covered with laurel leaves – and laurel was the tree special to Apollo, the god of poetry (and the patron god of the emperor). The poet also makes mention of times when he has faced danger from a falling tree (27), from the battle at Philippi (26) and from a sea voyage (28), just as in earlier books of the *Odes* he had described himself threatened by a wolf (I.22.9–16) and metamorphosed into a swan (II.20). This could strike the modern reader as manifestly ironic, just like his claim in *Odes* II.7 that Mercury saved his life at Philippi (see note on line 26 below), sending up the genre rather than making any serious claims for himself. It certainly sets up an aura of poetic self-consciousness which shows how this poet can beat the Greeks at their own game – and smile about it while doing so.

1–2 Calliope was the 'queen' of the Muses and later on was regarded as the patroness of epic poetry, and invoking her at the start of this poem establishes a clear link with the address to the Muse at the end (69–72) of the previous poem. Line 2 ends with two Greek words juxtaposed: the name Calliope (meaning something like 'beautiful voice') and the word **melos** meaning 'song' or 'tune', found only here in Horace. The peremptory tone of the two imperatives **dic age** is perhaps surprising in addressing a **regina** but the poet clearly enjoys a close relationship with his patroness, rather like that of Odysseus with the goddess Athena, and Horace had described himself (III.1.3) as the 'priest of the Muses'.

3–4 The poet widens the range of possible musical media: we had the pipe (**tibia**) in line 1, and now we have the voice (3), the lyre-strings (**fidibus**) and the **cithara** (4). These last two words both refer to the same instrument, the ancestor of the modern guitar, played with fixed strings on a solid base; the instrument was called *fides* in Latin and *lyra* or *cithara* in Greek. Horace's use of the two languages here is advertising that this poem is going to be a blend of the two cultures. The Muse has a voice which is 'clear/sharp' (**acuta**) and the lyre is credited with being the instrument of the god Apollo, here given his Greek name of Phoebus as in III.66. The combination of pipe, voice and lyre suggests the sort of choral lyric (as was composed by Pindar) rather than the monodic lyric of an Alcaeus or Sappho, and Horace is thus signalling that this is going to be a poem in the tradition of Pindar.

5–6 auditis is addressed possibly to the audience of this poem and suggests that the poet hears the voice of Calliope but that his audience do not – or else it is addressed to the Muses ('are you listening to me [and hearing my prayer] or is this all an illusion?'), with the poet presenting himself almost as a medium receiving messages from 'the other side'. The poet speculates on whether his inspiration is the result of his being deceived (**ludit**) by madness (**insania**) – although this madness is 'lovable' and thus pleasant. **audire** picks up **auditis** and there is a nice touch in the poet enjoying both his auditory illusion and also the visions of lovely landscapes in lines 6–8.

6–8 The Muses are commonly associated with natural haunts like springs and woods, and there is a theme in classical poetry of poetic inspiration as the spring of Castalia. The adjectives here pick up the idea of 'lovely' (**amabilis** 5) in **pios ... amoenae**, both coming at the end of successive lines: *pius* suggests that these are dedicated to the gods, while *amoenus* has the sense of 'pleasant'.

9–20 These lines describe a personal account of the poet as a child being saved by doves who laid foliage on his sleeping body and hid him from marauding snakes and bears. The language of this long sentence is strained and complex: we have a long first clause with hyperbaton of **fabulosae ... palumbes**, followed by two relative clauses (**quod ... quicumque**) and then two clauses with **ut**. This extended sentence gives the impression of rhapsodic, grand poetry inspired by the Muses.

9–13 fabulosae (9) agrees with **palumbes** at the end of line 12, a good example of hyperbaton, and the basic main sentence is: *palumbes texere me puerum*. The phrase in line 11 agrees with the **puerum.**

9 The sentence begins with emphasis on **me** to enhance the sequence of thought: the Muses are listening to me now because they always cherished me even when I was a child. The juxtaposition with **fabulosae** serves to enhance the poetic fantasy of what follows and the links between the poet and the material he deals with. Monte **Vulture** is a mountain in the Apulian district not far from Horace's birthplace of Venusia; the name suggests 'vulture' which is a nice contrast to the wood-pigeons which protect him in line 12.

10 'beyond the threshold of my nurse Apulia' is what the printed text seems to mean and is almost certainly based on a textual error. For one thing the scansion of **Apuliae** (as *ăpūlĭāe*) differs from the scansion of **Apulo** (*āpŭlō*) in the previous line; for another, the boy was within the territory of Apulia and not beyond it. We can read **nutricis** as a metaphor (Apulia my nurse) and **extra limen** does give the pleasing image of the boy wandering off the porch of the family home.

11 'tired out with play and with sleep' is excellent: the activity of playing made the child tired and then the sleep which followed made him drowsy.

12 palumbes are wood-pigeons which flock on Monte Vulture. The bird is associated with the goddess Venus, whose chariot is drawn by doves, and this is perhaps significant for a budding love-poet.

13 foret is the alternative form of *esset* (imperfect subjunctive of *sum*) and has consecutive force here – 'so that it was a marvel to all'. **quod** picks up the whole of the previous stanza as 'something which …'

14–16 The generalizing plural **quicumque** ('whoever' – i.e. all those who) leads on to names of some less familiar Italian places. Acherontia (Acerenza), Bantia (Banzi) and Forentum (Forenza) are all small places in the Apulian district near Venusia where Horace grew up. The listing of these names is interesting: on the one hand it confers greatness on places which did not enjoy fame until the poet immortalized them in his poetry – like the Bandusian spring in *Odes* III.13 – and on the other hand it moves sharply from the Greek to the decidedly Italian world, bringing the poetry of a Pindar to the humble local landscape. The places are also given some topographical colour: Acheruntia is perched high (**celsae**) like a bird's nest (**nidum**), Bantia has wooded glades (**saltus**) while low-lying (**humilis**) Forentum has rich (**pingue**) soil (**arvum**).

17–18 ut here means 'how' picking up from **mirum** in line 13 ('a marvel … how I slept'). The point of the foliage was presumably camouflage to protect the sleeping boy from animals. The ablative **tuto … corpore** is one of description and the **ab** follows naturally from **tuto** to mean 'with a body safe from …'. The **viperis** are the snakes which inhabit Italy, called 'black' to denote their poisonous danger as much as for their colour, while the bears need no qualifying adjective to show their danger. Italy had bears in its woodland in ancient times and bear-meat was eaten in Roman banquets (see e.g. Petronius 66, where Habinnas asks: 'if bears eat people, why should people not eat bears?').

18–19 texere in line 13 suggested a light covering: **premerer** now suggests a heavier coating of leaves, and the poet lists the different leaves used. **-que … -que …** joins the laurel and the myrtle, and both types of leaf are seen as **sacra** and have been **collata** to form the blanket. Laurel was the bush sacred to Apollo, god of poetry and prophecy, while myrtle was sacred to Venus.

20 The line sums up what has gone before with modest claims of his special status. The poet is 'not without' divine help from the Muses – a humble litotes – and even though he does not yet speak (**infans** derives from *in-fari* 'to be unable to speak' (see OLD s.v. 1)) he is already 'infused with spirit' (**animosus**) both in his courage at wandering alone and in his innate 'soul' which would one day deliver poems (like this one).

21 The poet addresses the Muses with their Italian name of **Camenae** and their name is framed by the repetition of **vester** suggesting that as he owes his life to them, they are central to his being and he belongs to them. The rest of the stanza lists a range of places where he might go to reinforce the idea that wherever he is he belongs to the Camenae. For this 'wherever I go' figure see Catullus XI.1–14.

21–4 The juxtaposition of **arduos / tollor** over the line-break strongly states the altitude of Horace's Sabine estate, on which see, for example, *Satires* II.6. The word **Sabinos** properly means 'the Sabines' but here means the area rather than the people in it. **Praeneste** (modern Palestrina) was also elevated and so 'cool'; this made it, like the Sabine estate, welcome during the hot summer months, as was **Tibur** (modern Tivoli) where Horace loved to go (*Epistles* I.7.45). **Baiae** was a seaside resort on the bay of Naples much frequented by the rich of Rome and notorious for both its conspicuous consumption and its louche lifestyle (OCD s.v. 'Baiae'). Again, the sea air would have been welcome (**placuere**).

25–8 In this stanza the poet lists three times when his life could have ended prematurely and credits the Muses with saving him to be a 'friend' (**amicum**) to their 'springs and dances'. The 'springs' in question include Castalia and Hippocrene, both famed for artistic inspiration. The theme of danger encountered and overcome, which is set up here, looks forward to the poet's adventurous future plans in lines 29–36.

26–7 Horace was on the losing side at the battle of Philippi in 42 BC when the forces of those who had assassinated Julius Caesar (Brutus and Cassius and others) fought against the forces of Caesar's henchman Antony and the young Octavian – who was to become the emperor Augustus. It might seem rash for the poet here to remind his emperor that he had once fought against him, but equally it could express confidence in the emperor's policy of *clementia* towards his former foes. The poet refers to the battle in *Odes* II.7.13–14 where he credits the god Mercury with saving him – a nice touch of poetic irony. The subject of the verb **exstinxit** is the **acies** which has been routed (**versa … retro**) but has not killed the poet, mainly because Horace threw away his shield and so escaped.

27 The 'cursed tree' (**devota … arbos**) fell and almost crushed Horace to death on his Sabine estate, as recounted in *Odes* II.13.

28 The third brush with death seems to have taken place on a sea voyage; Cape Palinurus is a promontory named after the hapless pilot of Aeneas' ship who fell overboard there (*Aeneid* VI.373). **Sicula … unda** is an instrumental ablative going with **exstinxit** (27).

29–36 The following two stanzas list six possible peoples for him to visit – all of them dangerous – to stress the poet's reliance on the help of the Muses for his safety in the future as in the past. He is so sure of their aid that he is 'willing' (**libens**) to visit these places and will be **inviolatus** throughout the journey: the two words nicely frame the travelogue. The poet brings out his mode of transport as a sailor (**navita**, the archaic form of *nauta*) on sea and a traveller (**viator**) on the land.

29–30 The poet's readiness to undertake the risk is enhanced by the juxtaposition over the line-break of **libens / insanientem** and by the descriptions of the places to be visited as raging waters and burning sand. The Bosphorus, a channel which links the Black Sea and the

Sea of Marmara, is personified as 'insane' both as a metaphor for the raging storms encountered there and also as a transferred epithet indicating that only a madman would risk this voyage. The 'burning sands' of the Assyrian shore refer probably to the Persian Gulf.

33 Britain was regarded as the furthest part of the world to the West, and by Horace's time Caesar had visited the islands but done little beyond seeing what was there. The Britons are said to be 'savage to guests' (**hospitibus feros**) perhaps because the Druids there were said to perform human sacrifice, as reported by Caesar (*Gallic Wars* VI.16).

34 The Concani were a notoriously fierce race in the north of Spain. They were said to sacrifice horses to their god of war and to drink the blood of the victims.

35–6 The Geloni were a fearsome Scythian tribe whose name suggests 'ice' (*gelu*) and who were renowned archers (cf. Virgil *Aeneid* VIII.725). The 'Scythian river' was the Tanais (Don) and was a byword for extreme cold: see III.10.1 where cold-hearted Lyce is imagined as living by the edge of the Tanais.

37–9 So far the poem has been entirely about Horace himself. Now he brings in Caesar (Augustus) as another man assisted by the Muses, who are the subject of the verb **recreatis** (40) (whose object is **Caesarem**). Caesar is described as 'lofty' or 'exalted' (**altum**), the troops as 'weary with military service' (**militia ... fessas**); and Caesar himself is 'seeking to end his toils' in a note of sympathy for the commander and his men. It was common practice for Roman commanders to settle their veteran soldiers on lands in the towns (**oppidis**) of Italy, as we hear in *Satires* II.2 and Virgil *Eclogues* I.

40 The 'Pierian cave' here symbolizes the idyllic place where the warrior Caesar may find rest and nourishment in literature. Pieria was in Macedonia, near Mt Olympus, and had been associated with the Muses since time immemorial (Hesiod *Works and Days* I).

41–2 'You give gentle advice and you rejoice in it once it is given, kindly ones'. **almae** derives from *alo* ('I feed') and is often used of nurturing goddesses (cf. Lucretius I.2). Horace does not specify the exact nature of the gentle advice given by the Muses to Caesar but we may assume that it refers to Caesar's efforts to pacify the Roman world after the civil wars which followed the battle of Actium in 31 BC. The line is scanned thus: *vōs lēnĕ cōnsīli(um) ĕt dătĭs ĕt dătō* with the third vowel of *consilium* treated as a consonant, which lengthens the previous syllable; this device ('synizesis') is also used at 6.6.

42 scimus engages the audience with the poet in a first-person plural verb ('we know') which enforces the consensus about the myth he is going on to discuss – a myth which will point a moral that force needs to be tempered if it is not to end in ruin. Jupiter has already in the Roman Odes (*Odes* III.1.5–8) been described as 'famous for his victory over the Giants'. **ut** here means 'how' as in line 17. **impios** marks out the Titans whom the poet conflates with the Giants. For the concept of *pietas* see **pios** at line 6.

42–8 The long sentence begins with the object (the Titans) before giving the verb (**sustulerit**) and only then telling us the subject, giving over an entire stanza to list and describe Jupiter's attributes without needing to name him. Horace talks about Titans in 43 but later on (49–58) switches to the Giants and the distinction clearly was not one the poet was concerned about.

42–3 The phrase **impios / Titanas immanemque turbam** is a hendiadys for the 'monstrous mob of the unholy Titans' – and the magnitude of the threat is conveyed by the expansive phrasing here.

44 There is a pleasing oxymoron in **sustulerit caduco** as the verb (which here means 'eliminated them') elsewhere indicates 'lifting up' while the adjective denotes 'falling down'.

45–8 The poet's eye scans the power of Jupiter from above (lands and seas) and then zooms in on the details of the cities of the living and the realms of the dead in a series of contrasting pairs (land vs sea, living vs dead, gods vs men) which are unified under the rule of the singular divine **unus**. **qui** here means *is qui* ('the one who …')

45–6 The earth is 'unmoving' as it is a solid land mass, whereas the sea is whipped up by the winds (**ventosum**) into movement. **temperat** ('controls') is more appropriate to the sea than the land.

47–8 The word **turmas** (which usually denotes a group of soldiers) is followed by the military term **imperio**. **unus** here has adjectival force ('he alone').

49 The previous stanza had made it seem easy for Jupiter to deal with the threat from the Titans – this one fills in the 'back story' with the pluperfect verb **intulerat** telling us what had happened to make this a real danger which was enough to terrify even Jupiter.

50 This details some of the more frightening aspects of the Titans and their allies. They were young (**iuventus**) and confident (**fidens**) in the strength of their arms (**bracchiis**) which reminds us that some of them (e.g. Briareus) had 100 hands. The word **horrida** ('bristling' or 'shaggy') connotes the forest of swirling arms.

51–2 The 'brothers' were Otus and Ephialtes who in the myth sought to tear up Mt Ossa to put it on top of Mt Olympus, and then to put Mt **Pelion** on top of Ossa in order to scale the heavens and unseat the gods. Olympus may be **opaco** as it was so high as to be clouded over or else simply as it was shrouded in leafage (cf. Virgil *Georgics* I.282). **imposuisse** literally means that the brothers sought 'to have put' the mountain in place but may simply be an example of the perfective aspect of the infinitive indicating the completed action.

53–8 The threat was real but not enough to overpower the might of the Olympian gods. The poet names a sequence of five Giants in one stanza, only to have them overcome by the single power of the aegis of Pallas, backed up by three other gods. There is good variation here: the sequence begins with **Typhoeus** simply named, followed by **Mimas** with a single word of description, followed by **Porphyrion** with a two-word descriptive ablative, followed by **Rhoetus** simply named and culminating in the five-word naming of **Enceladus**.

53 Typhoeus was half-man and half-dragon, whom Pindar describes as 'enemy of the gods, with one hundred heads, once nurtured in the famous Cilician cave – but now the rocks over Cyme … press on his hairy chest' (*Pythian* I.16–19). **Mimas** flung the island of Lemnos against the gods but was killed by Vulcan (cf. **avidus … Vulcanus** 58–9) with red-hot metal.

54 minaci … statu is an ablative of description ('with threatening pose'). **Porphyrion** was the king of the Giants who was destroyed (in one account by the bow of Apollo, in another by Jupiter and Hercules) after he tried to rape Juno.

55–6 Rhoetus was a Giant (cf. *Odes* II.19.23). **Enceladus** was a Giant whose battle with Pallas Athena became the subject of sculpture as on the temple of Apollo at Delphi, and who was buried under Mt Etna. Here he is a dynamic 'spear-thrower' (**iaculator**) – using torn up trees as his weapons. **audax** could stand for all these monsters and the theme of 'violence without wisdom' will be taken up later at line 65.

57–64 After the five named monsters the poet now lists four gods, culminating in Augustus' patron god **Apollo**. The theme of 'purity' is prominent here (the virginal goddess Pallas, the *matrona* Juno and Apollo using *rore puro* to wash his hair) and looks forward to the sexually immoral sinners whom we will meet in lines 70–80.

57 The 'aegis' is sometimes described as a weapon, sometimes a shield, or breastplate or cloak, and here the word **sonantem** ('echoing') suggests that it was a shield. Its use by Athene to terrify the enemy is attested in Homer *Odyssey* XXII.297–9.

58 possent is eloquent: not what the Giants did achieve but what 'could' they achieve, for all their forward rushing (**ruentes**).

58–64 To defeat the Giants Horace presents a further three gods culminating in the figure of **Apollo** who is given five lines to describe him.

58–9 Vulcan (Hephaistos in Greek) was the blacksmith god of fire, son of Juno who was the wife and sister of Jupiter. **avidus** suggests both 'greedy for battle' and also that fire is a greedy destructive force.

60 Apollo is the god of poetry as we have seen in line 4; but he is also a god of violence whose bow sends plague on to the Greek camp at the start of Homer's *Iliad* and who is often described in Homer as 'far-shooting' – Ovid (*Metamorphoses* I.441–4) paints a similar picture of the lethal archery of the god. Apollo was also Augustus' protecting patron god whose sanctuary at Actium was close to the scene of the great victory in 31 BC and to whom Augustus dedicated a temple on the Palatine Hill in 28 BC.

61–4 The image of **Apollo** here is conventional and drawn partly from Pindar *Pythian* III.39 where he is addressed as one who is 'lover of the

Castalian spring on Parnassus'. The Castalian spring on Mt Parnassus is useful here for washing the god's famous long hair. The language of this passage is remarkably pastoral: the god 'holds' (i.e. lives there as a controlling deity as as III.28.14) the 'thickets' of Lycia and the 'woods' of his birth, washing in a spring. **lavit** is third-person singular of the present tense of the archaic third conjugation verb *lavĕre* (later Latin has the verb as first conjugation *lavare*).

64 Patareus: Patara in Lycia had a temple of **Apollo** where he used to prophesy. Delos was the island of his birth (on Mt Cynthos). The whole stanza leads up to the climactic final word naming the god.

65-8 The poet generalizes with the kind of judgement which is common in the choral lyric of Pindar (see Introduction): violence which is restrained (**temperatam**) by judgement and purposeful is favoured by the gods, but mere brutality is doomed to disaster. Note the emphatic repetition of **vis … vim … vires** at the beginnings and end of lines.

65 mole ruit sua suggests an image of a building collapsing under its own mass. The following lines will, however, show that force like this is punished by third parties.

66-7 The 'extension' of controlled force is mirrored in the way the phrase itself is extended by enjambement.

67-8 vires is the plural of *vis* and is described in line 68 as 'moving every misdeed in its mind'. **idem** means literally 'the same ones' but here means 'they also … ˊ

69-70 Gyas was one of the Giants who tried to scale the heavens; he was flung into the underworld by the thunderbolts of Jupiter (cf. *Odes* II.17.14). Note here the immensity of the monster supported by the

compound adjective **centimanus** ('hundred-handed') followed by the
sonorous **sententiarum** in enjambement.

71 Orion was another of the Giants (and son of Terra) and was a famous
hunter who assaulted Diana. The word **temptator** here indicates that
his efforts were no more than that but were doomed to punishment
nonetheless. The juxtaposition of **Orion Dianae** represents verbally
the (attempted) closeness of their bodies.

72 Diana (Artemis in Greek) was dedicated to virginity and so
Orion was never likely to succeed. Her virgin status here is applied
to the arrow with which she subdued him and the term **virginea**
triumphantly emphasizes that Diana remained a *virgo*.

73–4 The order for translation is: *Terra, iniecta monstris suis, dolet*
('Earth, piled up on her own monsters, grieves'). The Giants were
buried under mountains such as Etna in Sicily. The wording of
dolet … maeretque partus indicates that Horace is thinking of the
personified **Terra** ('Mother Earth') who is lamenting her lost children.
The sentence is highly effective also with the use of **suis** ('her own
monsters') and the vivid image of the mother covering her dead
babies with herself. *luridus* denotes a sickly-yellow colour and is often
applied to the ghosts of the underworld.

75 Orcus, like Hades in Greek, means both the god of the underworld
and his realm.

75–80 peredit and **reliquit** are both perfect tenses and show that,
for all the long passage of time, the fire has not yet eaten up the
mountain and the bird has not yet left the liver, while the present
tense of **cohibent** shows that the chains still hold Pirithous even
now. All this brings out the eternal punishment to which they were
condemned.

77 *incontinens* indicates one who cannot contain (*continere*) his appetites and corresponds to the Greek term *akrasia* (discussed in book 7 of Aristotle's *Nicomachean Ethics*). Tityos was another of the Giants, who tried to rape Leto and so was punished by her children Apollo and Artemis. He is seen as a byword for excessive sexual passion in Lucretius III.992–4.

78–9 The bird was applied as a guard to his wickedness (**nequitiae** is dative) – that is, the vulture was sent to watch over him (and eat his liver) because of his wickedness. The legend of the liver being eaten at by birds reminds the reader of the legend of Prometheus to whom similar torments were given. The liver was regarded as the seat of emotions (e.g. Juvenal I.45, XI.187) and eating the liver was something which the grim Hecuba wishes to do to her son's killer Achilles in Homer's *Iliad* (XXIV.212–13).

79–80 trecentae is literally '300' but here denotes any unfeasibly large number. Pirithous was king of the Lapiths whose crime was to go down to the underworld with Theseus and try to abduct Proserpina, the daughter of Ceres and wife of the god of the underworld – hence his ironic title here of 'lover'. Pirithous was seized by Pluto and bound to a rock. The theme of sexual incontinence is one which Ode VI is going to pursue in more contemporary terms.

6

This is a deeply pessimistic poem, at least on the surface. The message – that society is going to Hell in a handcart and things will only get worse – might seem surprising in a collection which is urging moral and social regeneration, but the implication of the doom and gloom is that Augustus' regeneration is our (only) chance to avoid this fate.

The ode is made up of twelve stanzas divided into three groups of four.

1–16 Rome needs to keep the gods on side as she has faced near disaster in the recent past.

17–32 Sexual immorality is rife in Rome.

33–48 People today are not as they were, and things will only get worse.

The ode thus looks to the past in the first and the last sections, while the central panel of the triptych looks at the world around it almost in a satirical mode of vivid disapproval.

The tone is on the surface religious to a surprising degree. Our misfortunes are (it is asserted) the result of our sin, and future prosperity depends on our repenting and improving our ways. The political side is heavily marked also, given that Augustus boasted that he restored eighty-two temples of the gods (*Res Gestae* XX.4: cf. Livy IV.20.7) and he had already dedicated a temple to Apollo in 28 BC. Military disappointments are also linked to ritual failures (9–12) and the war at Actium is alluded to as a near-miss (**paene**) for the forces of the East (13–16), as the Romans were too busy fighting each other.

The poem then veers from the (inter)national to the private sphere of domestic morality and the sexual misbehaviour of the current generation. In the poem the wife's motive is lust, the husband's motive is greed and both are equally condemned.

The poet is clearly glancing at a range of ideas which would soon become enshrined in the 'moral and social legislation' of Augustus, the main articles of which were as follows: marriage was made compulsory for men between the ages of twenty-five and sixty and for women between twenty and fifty; to make this easier, Augustus allowed men who were not senators to marry freedwomen. A woman who was divorced had to remarry within six months and widows had to remarry within a year (*lex Julia de maritandis ordinibus*). The purpose of this was presumably to raise the birth rate amongst the upper classes – see Dio's account of his speech to the unmarried men (Dio 56.6–9) for a flavour of the rhetoric behind the legislation – and there were some (to us) draconian restrictions on marriage with the so-called *infames* (gladiators, pimps, convicts and actors) who were not permitted to marry any but their own kind.

Adultery had up till that point been a private matter dealt with by the family: Augustus set up a permanent court (*quaestio perpetua*) to try cases of wifely infidelity and the penalty was exile to distant islands for both the errant wife and her lover, as well as confiscation of property. Any husband who turned a blind eye to his wife's adultery was to be arraigned on suspicion of colluding with the immorality (*lex Julia de adulteriis coercendis*), while a woman found to have committed adultery was ruined – she had to cease wearing the *stola* and had to wear the *toga* of a prostitute. Many no doubt became prostitutes to survive.

The legislation was not in fact passed until 18 BC (five years after the publication of the *Odes*) so the poet's use of this material here is more corroborating what must have been discussed in the imperial court rather than approving of laws which had already been announced in public. In the poem the wicked adulterer is the lustful unfaithful wife and her conniving husband is clearly pimping her out to a wealthy man – a man who is lower-class and/or a foreigner. This combines the sexual with more than a touch of snobbery when we read the disdain the poet brings to the phrase *seu vocat institor / seu navis Hispanae magister / dedecorum pretiosus emptor* (30–2).

Little if any *moral* disapproval is expressed against the wife's lover in fact; he is simply buying a product much as Horace himself recommends in *Satires* I.2.101–19. Suetonius (*Life of Augustus* 69) tells us that Augustus himself was well known as an adulterer – although in his case it was more to find out via pillow talk the thoughts of his potential enemies rather than motivated by lust. A husband could of course be unfaithful to his wife with his slaves or with prostitutes and freedwomen without threatening the family bloodline and this 'double standard' is accepted without comment by the poet: once again, the criticism is aimed at the feeble or corrupt husband who cannot keep his wife in order rather than the hot-blooded lover who takes advantage of this, and this is a theme of Roman love poetry (e.g. Catullus 17, Ovid *Amores* I.4, 2.7).

1 maiorum is from *maiores* 'ancestors' and the argument is that 'you' (**Romane** in the next line, the anonymous 'Roman' addressee of the poem) will pay for the sins of the ancestors even though you personally are not to blame for them. This theme – Adam ate the apple but we get the stomach ache – underlies many tragic tales involving family curses. For Horace's use of **Romane** see Virgil *Aeneid* VI.852.

2–4 The poet refers to the physical sites associated with the gods in three different ways (**templa ... aedes ... simulacra**) with ascending levels of description attached to them. The divine sites are first referred to simply as **templa** but then described as 'falling-down abodes of the gods' and finally as 'images foul with black smoke'. **labentes** describes the 'slipping' or 'falling down' of the buildings.

5 The construction is thus: 'because you conduct yourself (**te ... geris**) as less important (**minorem**) than the gods (**dis** – ablative of comparison), you rule.' The paradox is that man's subservience to the divine gives him power over others. The gods confirm men in power, and material success proves the favour of the gods; the obverse is clear from *Odes* III.2.26–9 where the poet refuses to go into a boat with a guilty man for fear of divine punishment hitting them both.

6 There is a pleasing balance here between **hinc** and **huc** and between **principium** and **exitum**. The terms **hinc** and **huc** here are to be understood metaphorically – 'derive every beginning from this (obedience to the gods) and make this the end'. The Roman addressed in **Romane** (2) is still the subject of the imperative **refer. principium, huc** is scanned *prīncĭpĭ(um) hūc* with synizesis as at IV.41.

7–8 The adjectival term **neglecti** explains the whole sentence: it is because they gods have been ignored that they have given misfortune. **Hesperiae** is literally 'the Western Land' and here indicates Italy.

9 Parthia had been a target for Roman armies in the recent past and was the site of several battles which went badly for Roman forces, including a notorious case (Carrhae in 53 BC) where the general Crassus, according to Cicero (*de Divinatione* II.84) ignored the omens on his journey there whereby the fig-seller advertising his Caunian figs ('*Caunias!*') was heard to be advising '*cave ne eas*' (beware of going). The Parthians are listed in reverse chronological order: Pacorus (a Parthian prince) defeated the forces of Antony's lieutenant L. Decidius Saxa in 40 BC after the latter made an unwise move on Palmyra; while **Monaeses** (the Parthian commander) crushed Oppius Statianus in 36 BC when Antony invaded Parthia.

10 The key phrase is **non auspicatos** which explains the violent verb **contudit** which follows it.

11–12 There is vivid description here as we see the Parthian 'grinning' (**renidet** – also used by Catullus of a silly grin (39.2)) to have added our plunder to his 'little neckbands' which are dainty and effeminate.

13 seditionibus here must refer to the internecine strife which marred the last century of the Roman Republic: the strife between Marius and Sulla, leading to the dictatorship of the latter, followed by the strife by and between the members of the first Triumvirate

(Crassus, Pompey and Julius Caesar) followed by the Civil War of
49 BC between Caesar and Pompey which ended in the dictatorship
of Caesar. His assassination in 44 BC led to fresh wars between his
successors Octavian and Mark Antony, which ended in the defeat of
the latter at Actium in 31 BC and the establishment of the principate
of Octavian/Augustus. Horace, looking back on this catalogue of
blood and misery, sees it as a close-run thing (**paene**). There is a good
deal of exaggeration in Horace's language – the 'Ethiopian' (from the
extreme south in Africa) and the 'Dacian' (from the remote north on
the Danube) did not threaten to attack Rome itself – but this well
expresses the fear of what might have been.

13–16 Here the reference is to the battle of Actium: Dacian archers
(described here as 'better with flying arrows' (line 16)) served under
Antony, and the 'Ethiopian' refers to the Egyptian troops who manned
Cleopatra's fleet (**classe** line 15).

17–32 The second third of the poem gives us a moralizing picture
of sexual immorality as another explanation of the disasters which
threaten Rome. The poet has already told us that the gods have given
us misfortune when neglected (lines 7–8) – he now shows us the
pollution in family values.

17 'Ages fertile in sin' is an elliptical phrase denoting the duration
and the quality of the misconduct. **fecunda** normally refers to
procreative power and the sardonic twist here is that these times are
only producing sin rather than the masculine offspring of days gone
by (37–8). For **culpae** used in this sense see Virgil *Aeneid* IV.172.

17–18 The target of the pollution is the threefold **nuptias ... genus ...
domos**: marriage (and therefore) the race itself and homes/families.
Anything which threatens the integrity of marriage will (the poet
asserts) pollute the bloodline and the stable homes on which Roman

inheritance depended. **inquinavere** is a strong word denoting the dirtying and polluting effect of one thing on another and starts the motif of liquid imagery which continues with **fonte derivata ... fluxit** in lines 19–20.

19–20 'Disaster, channeled from this source, has flowed onto the fatherland and its people.' **hoc fonte** refers back to the **culpae** of line 17 and there is a nice progression as the initial spring (**fonte**) ends up flooding the landscape.

21–32 These three stanzas focus on the behaviour of the young woman; she is unmarried (**virgo**) but being trained in lines 21–4, then married but promiscuously adulterous in lines 25–32. The criticism is also levelled at the husband who is fully aware (**conscio**) of what she is doing and actually telling her to do it (**iussa**).

21 'Ionic movements' refers to dancing steps which originated in Ionia (the western edge of Turkey inhabited by Greeks and with a reputation for luxury). Dancing was something which slave girls would do and which was suspect in a freeborn woman, frowned at in a married lady (cf. Fortunata's dancing of the *cordax* in Petronius 52.8). The juxtaposition of **doceri gaudet** is also significant: decent girls would be unwilling to compromise their modesty thus, but this girl is happy to be taught the steps.

22 The girl is unmarried but no longer a child (**matura**). **fingitur artibus** is delightfully ambiguous: she is being 'shaped' both *by* the arts she is practising and also *for* them; the noun *figura* is linked to this verb and the poet thus gently alludes to her developing a physical shape to match her abilities.

23–4 incestos is *in-castos* (un-chaste: cf. III.19) and **meditatur** shows that she is already (**iam nunc**) planning her career as an adulteress even before she is married: **amores** often has this sense of 'love-affairs'. **de tenero … ungui** means literally 'down from her tender fingernail' and two interpretations have been argued: one is that it derives from the Greek phrase 'from soft nails' and means 'from earliest childhood', but this is rendered improbable as the girl is now **matura** (22) and there is strong emphasis (**iam nunc**) on the fact that this is current behaviour. More plausibly the phrase means 'with her whole being', 'heart and soul' analogous to the Greek *ex onuchon* ('from the nails') which has precisely this meaning; there is something nicely ironic about the poet borrowing a Greek phrase to describe a girl who is borrowing lascivious Greek dancing moves. The addition of the adjective **tenero** is typical of Horace – the term is often used of a sexually attractive girl (e.g. *Odes* I.1.26, *Satires* I.2.81, Catullus XX.15, 61.100, Ovid *Metamorphoses* XI.153).

25–6 mox indicates the rapid passage of time and the words **adulteros … mariti** suggest that the **virgo** (22) is now married. **iuniores** means 'younger' and suggests that her husband is older than she would have preferred, hinting that her motivation is simply lust. Her seeking out of lovers reminds us of the activities of Clodia according to Cicero *pro Caelio* 35–6, but this girl is both a voracious vamp and also the sex-worker of a corrupt husband (29–32).

26 vina gives us the imagery of the *convivium* ('party') with its atmosphere of wine, women and song. For the vignette of the dinner party where a wife is with her husband and her lover see Ovid *Amores* I.4 but (unlike in the Ovid poem) the tables are turned here as the husband is fully in on the activities (**conscio** line 29) and indeed the wife does not choose her partners. Interestingly, a similar story is told in Suetonius (*Augustus* 69.1) of the young Augustus who once took the wife of an ex-consul from a dinner party into the bedroom and then brought her back to the table 'with hair a mess and ears glowing'.

26–8 The poet's indignation is brought out well. The pleasures are 'forbidden' (**impermissa**), granted in the darkness (**luminibus remotis**) and in a hurry (**raptim**) perhaps to get through as many as she can in the time available. The word **gaudia** is richly ironic in the context.

29–32 The previous stanza was bad – but things are now made worse by the husband's organizing of it all. She is commanded (**iussa**) in public (**coram**) by her own husband to service the men – and they turn out to be foreigners and lower-class merchants. The **institor** was a pedlar or travelling salesman, while the mention of the 'Spanish sea-captain' adds a touch of xenophobia to the disgust. Pedlars and sailors were often paired as the customers of prostitutes (e.g. *Epodes* XVII.20) and pedlars in particular were regarded as sexually loose (e.g. Ovid *Ars Amatoria* I.421, *Remedium Amoris* 306). The sea-captain may well have been the owner of his own ship and therefore wealthy but Horace taps into the Roman upper-class distaste for trade with the scornful term **dedecorum pretiosus emptor. pretiosus** is elsewhere used of the goods themselves ('expensive') and the sense is double here: he is a prodigal spender, but this sort of behaviour will prove costly to everyone. There is also irony in the term **magister** which means 'master' (and so captain) of the ship; here he shows his mastery over another man's wife.

33 non his makes for a strong start to the stanza: it was not parents like this who produced the great Romans of the past. It also casts a gentle query about the sort of offspring which promiscuous sexual behaviour of wives will produce.

34–6 A short trio of famous Roman conquests from the 'glory years' of the mid-Republican rise to power in the Mediterranean to prove Roman past greatness, with some telling imagery: the

seas were 'stained with Punic blood' when C. Duilius defeated the
Carthaginians at Mylae (260 BC) and later on when Lutatius Catulus
besieged Drepana in 242 BC, both events taking place in the first
Punic War (264–241 BC). The imagery of blood staining the sea is
also used at *Odes* II.1.35, II.12.3, Juvenal X.185–6 and here the image
plays on the associations of Phoenicia and the purple dye which it
famously produced. Pyrrhus of Epirus invaded Italy in 280 BC and
his ruinous victories coined the term 'Pyrrhic victory'; Antiochus III
was defeated by Scipio Africanus at Magnesia in 190 BC and his title
'the Great' is given a more poetic turn with the adjective **ingentem**
whose grandeur magnifies the scale of the victory over him. The verb
cecīdit is from *caedo* and has the violent sense 'hack down'. Hannibal
(247–182 BC) was the great Carthaginian general whose leadership in
the second Punic War against Rome almost brought disaster to the
world, according to the Romans (e.g. Lucretius III.833–7) and who
fully deserves the epithet **dirum**. He was finally defeated at the battle
of Zama in 202 BC (Livy XXX.29–35). The list is not in chronological
order, but ends appropriately with the greatest threat to Rome.

37–44 The poet ascribes the greatness of the former generations
to their rustic upbringing and consequent toughness. Romans –
especially urban types – had a tendency to romanticize the life of the
countryside and see it as more healthy both physically and morally:
see for instance the town mouse and the country mouse in *Satires* II.6,
and cf. *Epode* II, Virgil *Georgics* II.458–62, Juvenal *Satire* XI.142–60.

37 Note the emphasis on the rugged masculinity of the offspring in
the alliterative **mascula militum**.

38–40 The skills taught are agricultural ('turning the clods of earth
with Samnite mattocks') rather than military, although no doubt (as
in the famous tale of Quinctius Cincinnatus who left his ploughing to

become dictator, assemble an army, defeat the enemy and then return to his plough) the skills were transferable. **docta** reminds us of **doceri** in line 21 and the contrast between the **virgo** (22) and these young men is developed as the female working for the male husband (29–30) and being bought by other men now becomes a picture of males working for a strict female (**severae / matris**), the artificial lights being put out in 28 replaced by the natural sunset of 41–4.

40–1 The young men cut logs (**fustes**) and carry them to make firewood.

41–4 This stanza has the sun as its subject; as the sun departs it 'changes the shadows of the mountains', suggesting that the wood is being brought down from the mountain to the homestead in the valley. Less obviously, the sun 'takes the yokes off' the tired oxen – that is, the men remove the yokes once the sun has gone down. For the link between sunset and unyoking oxen see Homer *Odyssey* IX.58. The evening is the 'welcome time' (**amicum / tempus**) to all and the choice of *amicus* is charged for a Roman audience with suggestions of alliance and harmony. Sunset is a very effective closural motif, as at the end of Virgil *Eclogue* I. The subjunctives **mutaret** and **demeret** are most likely indefinite and frequentative ('whenever (as often happens)') but it has been suggested that they represent the words of the mother.

44 The sun is personified as riding away in his chariot such as that driven by Phaethon in Ovid's famous account (*Metamorphoses* II.1–366).

45 The passage of time is costly (**damnosa**) and has diminished everything; the poet begins his final stanza of this last in the series of Roman Odes with a stern rhetorical question, picking up the idea of daytime from the previous stanza and turning it into a pessimistic generalization.

46–8 The final three lines diminish in length and reduce in number of words (5, then 4, then 2) mirroring the inevitable weakening of the race. Our parents were worse than *their* parents (our **avis**), only to produce us (**nos**) who are more worthless still, doomed to produce offspring which is even more faulty. The inevitable decline is at odds with the more optimistic opening of the poem which encouraged Romans to rebuild temples and stop the neglect of the gods which had caused disaster in the past, and it is tempting to argue (with some scholars) that there is a concealed condition attached to this final stanza; things will certainly continue to decline unless we do something to stop it and sign up to a programme of moral regeneration.

Vocabulary

While there is no Defined Vocabulary List for A Level, words in the OCR Defined Vocabulary List (DVL) for AS Level are marked with * so that students can quickly see the vocabulary with which they should be particularly familiar, although the meanings given in this book are not necessarily the same as the ones in the DVL, as this vocabulary is tailored to this text.

This vocabulary lists every word in the text. Nouns are listed with their genitive singular, and verbs are listed with all their four principal parts. Adjectives are listed with the endings of the different genders (e.g. **bonus -a -um**) except where the three genders are the same in the nominative where the genitive is listed (e.g. **iners, inertis**).

*ab (+ ablative)	from, away from
*abdo, abdere, abdidi, abditum	to hide
*abeo, abire, abivi, abitum	to leave, depart from
*acer acris acre	hard, fierce (with *militia* 2.2)
Acheron -ontis, m	Acheron (a river in the Underworld: 3.16)
Acherontia -ae, f	Acherontia (a town: 4.14)
Achivus -a -um	Greek (3.27)
*acies, aciei, f	battle-line
acutus -a -um	clear-sounding (4.3)
*ad (+ accusative)	to, towards
*addo, addere, addidi, additum	to join (2.30), to set, apply (4.78)
adiicio, adiicere, adiecisse, adiectum	to add to

adscribo, adscribere, adscripsi, adscriptum	to enrol (3.35)
adulter -i, m	adulterer, lover
adultera -ae, f	an adulteress
adultus -a -um	grown up, fully grown
aedes, aedis, f	shrine (6.3)
aegis, aegidis, f	aegis (shield of Minerva: 4.57)
aeneus -a -um	made of bronze
aequor, aequoris, n	sea
*aequus, aequa, aequum	even-handed, fair (4.48)
aetas, aetatis, f	age, time
Aethiops, Aethiopis, m	Ethiopian (6.14)
Aetne -es, f	Etna (volcanic mountain: 4.76)
Afer, Afri, m	African
*age!	come now! (imperative of **ago:** 4.1)
*agmen, agminis, n	column of soldiers, warfare (2.9)
*ago, agere, egi, actum	to spend (time: 2.5), to lead on (6.44)
ales, alitis, m/f	bird (3.61, 4.78)
almus -a -um	nurturing, kindly
*altus -a -um	exalted, lofty
amabilis, -e	pleasant, lovable
amator, amatoris, m	lover
*amice (adverb)	as a friend (2.1)
*amicus -i, m	friend
amnis, amnis, m	stream, river
amoenus -a -um	charming, pleasant
*amor, amoris, m	love
*an (conjunction)	or

*angustus -a -um	tight, restricted (2.1)
animosus -a -um	spirited (4.20)
*animus -i, m	heart, innermost feelings
antecedo, antecedere, antecessi, antecessum	to go before, to go in front
Antiochus -i, m	Antiochus (king of Syria: 6.36)
antrum, antri, n	cave
Apollo, Apollinis, m	Apollo (a god)
Apulia -ae, f	Apulia (4.10)
Apulus -a -um	Apulian
*aqua -ae, f	water
arbitrium, arbitrii, n	authority (6.40)
*arbos, arboris, f	tree
arcanus -a -um	secret, hidden
arcus, arcūs, m	bow (used in archery)
ardor, ardoris, m	heat, passion
arduus -a -um	lofty, steep
Argivus -a -um	Argive (3.67)
*arma, armorum, n.pl.	weapons
armentum -i, n	herd
*ars, artis, f	skill (6.22), virtue (3.9)
arvum -i, n	field, ploughland
arx, arcis, f	citadel
asper, aspera, asperum	rough
Assyrius -a -um	Assyrian
ater, atra, atrum	black
attingo, attingere, attigi, attactum	to reach, attain
auctor, auctoris, m	builder, producer (3.66)
*audax, audacis	bold, daring
*audio, audire, audivi, auditum	to hear
Augustus -i	Augustus (Roman emperor)

aura -ae, f	breeze
aurum -i, n	gold
auspicatus -a -um	blessed with good auspices (6.10)
Auster, Austri, m	the south wind
***aut**	or
avidus -a -um	greedy, eager
avis, avis, f	bird
avitus -a -um	ancestral
Bacchus, -i, m	Bacchus
Baiae, Baiarum, f.pl.	Baiae (fashionable Roman bathing resort)
Bantinus -a -um	of Bantia (a town: 4.15)
beatus -a -um	happy, fortunate, wealthy
bellicosus -a -um	warlike
bello, bellare, bellavi, bellatum	to wage war
***bellum, i**, n	war
***bibo, bibere, bibi**	to drink
***bis** (adverb)	twice
bos, bovis, m/f (dat/abl plural: *bobus* 6.43)	ox, cow
Bosphorus -i, m	the Bosphorus
bracchium, bracchii, n	arm
Britannus -a -um	British
bustum -i, n	tomb
caducus -a um	falling
***caedes, caedis**, f	slaughter, carnage
caedo, caedere, cecīdi, caesum	to cut down, slay (6.35)
***caelum, -i**, n	heavens, sky
Caesar, Caesaris, m	Caesar (4.37)
Calliope -ēs, f	Calliope (Muse of lyric poetry: 4.2)
Camena -ae, f	Muse
***capio, capere, cepi, captum**	to take, to take prisoner

Capitolium, Capitolii, n	The Capitol and the temple of Jupiter on it (3.42)
Castalia -ae, f	Castalia (fountain on Mt Parnassus: 4.61)
castus -a -um	chaste, pure
catena -ae, f	chain
caterva -ae, f	troop, band
catulus -i, m	puppy
***celo, celare, celavi, celatum**	to hide
***celer, celeris, celere**	swift
celsus -a -um	lofty, raised high
centimanus -a -um	with 100 hands
Ceres, Cereris, f	Ceres (goddess of agriculture and corn: 2.26)
chorus -i, m	chorus, band of dancers
cithara -ae, f	lyre, harp
***civis, civis**, m	citizen
***clades, cladis**, f	disaster
classis -is, f	fleet of ships
claudo, claudere, clausi, clausum	to shut
coetus -ūs, m	gathering, throng
***cogo, cogere, coegi, coactum**	to force
cohibeo, cohibere, cohibui, cohibitum	to restrain, check
***cohors, cohortis**, f	cohort (a unit of soldiers)
collum -i, n	neck
Concanus -a -um	Concanian (a member of the Concani tribe: 4.34)
condisco, condiscere, condidici	to learn thoroughly
***confero, conferre, contuli, collatum**	to collect, gather together
***coniunx, coniugis**, m/f	spouse
conscius -a -um	fully aware, conniving

consilior, consiliari, consiliatus sum	to consult together (3.17)
*consilium, consilii, n	advice (4.41), judgement, thought (4.65)
*contra (+ accusative)	against
contundo, contundere, contudi, contūsum	to beat, crush
convenio, convenire, convēni, conventum (+ dative)	to agree with, be suited to
coram (adverb)	openly, publicly
*corpus, corporis, n	body
crinis -is, m	hair
cruentus -a -um	bloody
*culpa -ae, f	misconduct, sin
*cum	when, since
currus -ūs, m	chariot
*custos, custodis, m	guard, warder
Dacus -i, m	a Dacian
damno, damnare, damnavi, damnatum	to condemn, doom
damnosus -a -um	destructive, harmful
*de	from (6.24)
debacchor, debacchari, debacchatus sum	to rage to exhaustion, to burn out
decorus -a -um	honourable (2.13)
dedecus, dedecoris, n	disgrace, shame (6.32)
*deleo, delere, delevi, deletum	to destroy
delictum -i, n	crime, sin
Delius -a -um	Delian (4.64)
demo, demere, dempsi, demptum	take off, remove
derivo, derivare, derivavi, derivatum	to channel (a stream: 6.19)
*descendo, descendere, descendi, descensum	to come down
desero, deserere, deserui, desertum	to desert, abandon (2.32)
*desino, desinere, desivi, desitum	to stop, cease

destituo, destituere, destitui, destitutum	to cheat of (+ ablative of the thing withheld: 3.21)
***deus, dei**, m	god
devoveo, devovere, devōvi, devōtum	to curse (4.27)
***dextra -ae**, f	right hand
Diana -ae, f	Diana (a goddess: 4.71)
***dico, dicere, dixi, dictum**	to say
***dies -ei**, m/f	day
Diespiter -tris, m	the god Jupiter (2.29)
***dirus -a -um**	deadly, dread
divus -i	god (3.18, 4.47), the open sky (2.5)
***do, dare, dedi, datum**	to give
***doceo, docere, docui, doctum**	to teach
***doleo, dolere, dolui, dolitum**	mourn, grieve
domo, domare, domui, domitum	to subdue
***domus -ūs** (acc. pl. *domos*), f	home, house
donec	until (6.2)
dono, donare, donavi, donatum	to give (6.27)
***dormio, dormire, dormivi, dormitum**	to sleep
***duco, ducere, duxi, ductum**	to draw out (3.29), to drink (3.34), to lead (3.63)
dulcis -e	sweet
***dum** (+ subjunctive)	so long as, provided that
dumetum -i, n	thicket
***dux, ducis**, m	leader, chief
***ego, mei**	I, me
eheu!	alas!
eligo, eligere, elēgi, electum	to choose
***eloquor, eloqui, elocutus sum**	to speak aloud, declare
emptor, emptoris, m	buyer
Enceladus -i, m	Enceladus (a Giant: 4.56)
enitor, eniti, enisus sum	to strive

*eques, equitis, m	cavalry-soldier
equinus -a -um	of a horse
*equus -i, m	horse
*erro, errare, erravi, erratum	to wander, roam
*et	and
Europe -ēs, f	Europe (3.47)
evello, evellere, evelli, evulsum	to tear up
*ex (+ ablative)	from
ex quo	from the time when
excīdo, excīdere, excīdi, excīsum	to cut down
exiguus -a -um	meagre
exitus -ūs, m	end
expers, expertis (+ genitive)	devoid of, lacking in
exstinguo, exstingere, exstinxi, exstinctum	to wipe out, destroy
exsul, exsulis, m	an exile
extendo, extendere, extendi, extentum	to spread, extend
*extra (+ accusative)	beyond
fabulosus -a -um	fabled, legendary
famosus -a -um	notorious, infamous
fatalis -e	sent by fate, destined
fatigo, fatigare, fatigavi, fatigatum	to make tired
fatum -i, n	fate
fecundus -a -um (+ genitive)	productive of, prolific in
fera -ae, f	wild beast
ferio, ferire	to strike, hit
*fero, ferre, tuli, latum	to carry
*ferox, ferocis	fierce
ferus -a -um	savage, cruel
fessus -a -um (+ ablative)	weary of (4.38)
*fidelis -e	faithful
fides, -is, f	string of a musical instrument (4.4)

*fido, fidere, fisus sum (+ dative/ablative)	to trust in, have confidence in
fingo, fingere, finxi, fictum	to mould, shape (6.22)
finio, finire, finivi, finitum	to end
fluo, fluere, fluxi, fluctum	to flow
*foedus -a -um	filthy (6.4)
fons, fontis, m	fountain, spring
*forem = essem	(imperfect subjunctive of *sum*)
Forentum -i, n	Forentum (a small town 4.16)
formido, formidare, formidavi, formidatum	to dread
*fortis -e	strong, brave
*fortuna -ae, f	destiny, fortune
fragilis -e	fragile, frail (of a boat: 2.28)
*frango, frangere, fregi, fractum	to break
*frater, fratris, m	brother
fraudulentus -a -um	cheating
frigidus -a -um	chilly, cold
frons, frondis, f	leaf, foliage
fugax, fugacis	running away
*fugio, fugere, fūgi, fugitum	to flee
fulgeo, fulgere, fulsi	to shine
fulmen, fulminis, n	thunderbolt
fulmino, fulminare, fulminavi, fulminatum	to wield the thunderbolt
fumus -i, m	smoke
fustis -is, m	log
*gaudeo, gaudere, gavisus sum	to rejoice (4.42), be happy to (+ infinitive: 6.21)
*gaudium, gaudii, n	joy

Geloni, Gelonorum, m.pl.	the Geloni (4.35)
*genus, generis, n	race, family
*gero, gerere, gessi, gestum	
(+ reflexive pronoun)	to behave (6.5)
gestio, gestire, gesti(v)i, gestitum	to be eager
gleba -ae, f	lump of earth, clod
gratus -a -um	pleasing, welcome
*gravis -e	harsh, unsparing (of
	anger: 3.30)
Gyas -ae, m	Gyas (a Giant: 4.69)
Hadria, -ae, f	the Adriatic Sea (3.5)
Hannibal, Hannibalis, m	Hannibal (Carthaginian
	leader: 6.36)
harena -ae, f	sand
*hasta -ae, f	spear
Hectoreus -a -um	belonging to Hector (3.28)
Hercules -is, m	Hercules (a hero: 3.9)
Hesperia -ae, f	Hesperia (6.8)
*hic, haec, hoc	this
*hinc (adverb)	from here
Hispanus -a -um	Spanish
*honor, honoris, f	honour
horrendus -a -um (gerundive	
of *horreo* as adjective)	dreadful
horridus -a -um	bristling, shaggy (of the
	Giants: 4.50)
*hospes, hospitis, m	house-guest (3.26),
	stranger (4.33)
hosticus -a -um	of the enemy
*huc (adverb)	to this place
humanus -a -um	human, mortal
humilis -e	low-lying (4.16)
*humus -i, f	earth, ground

iaculator, iaculatoris, m	spear-thrower
*iam	by now
iam nunc	already (6.23)
*idem, eadem, idem	the same
iecur, iecoris, n	the liver
igneus -a -um	fiery
*ignis -is, m	fire
Ilion -i, n	Troy
illabor, illabi, illapsus sum	fall, collapse (3.7)
*ille, illa, illud	that
imbellis -e	cowardly, unwarlike
immanis -e	monstrous
immeritus -a -um	guiltless, undeserving (6.1)
imminuo, imminuere, imminui, imminūtum	to reduce, make smaller
impavidus -a -um	fearless
*impero, imperare, imperavi, imperatum	command, rule (6.5)
*imperium -ii, n	power, authority
impermissus -a -um	illicit (6.27)
*impetus -ūs, m	attack
impius -a -um	impious (4.42)
impono, imponere, imposui, impositum	pile upon (4.52, 4.76)
*in + ablative	in, on
*in + accusative	into
incestus -a -um	impure, guilty (2.30, 3.19) obscene (6.23)
incontinens, incontinentis	insatiable (4.77)
indocilis -e	unteachable, untamed
*ineo, inire, ini(v)i	to enter
iners, inertis	unmoving, inert (4.45)

infans, infantis	infant, child
infero, inferre, intuli, illatum	I bring to
inficio, inficere, infeci, infectum	to stain (6.34)
***ingens, ingentis**	huge
iniicio, iniicere, inieci, iniectum	throw upon (4.73)
inquietus -a -um	restless (3.5)
inquino, inquinare, inquinavi,	
inquinatum	to stain, defile
insania -ae, f	madness
insanio, insanire, insani(v)i, insanitum	to be mad
instans, instantis (participle	
from *insto*)	threatening (3.3)
institor, institoris, m	salesman, pedlar
insulto, insultare, insultavi, insultatum	to trample on
intaminatus -a -um	unsullied (2.18)
integer, integra, integrum	pure (2.30), virginal,
	untainted (4.70)
***inter** + accusative	between, amongst
inultus -a -um	unavenged, safe from
	punishment
inviolatus -a -um	unharmed
invisus -a -um	hated, hateful
iocosus -a -um	cheerful, humorous
Ionicus -a -um	Ionian (6.21)
***ira -ae, f**	anger
irrepertus -a -um	undiscovered
***iter, itineris, n**	journey, course
itero, iterare, iteravi, iteratum	to repeat
***iubeo, iubere, iussi, iussum**	to order
***iudex, iudicis, m**	judge
iugum -i	yoke
iunior, iunioris	younger
Iuppiter, Iovis, m	Jupiter (god: 3.6)

Iuno, Iunonis, f	Juno (goddess: 3.18)
ius, iuris, n	law, rights (3.44)
***iustus -a -um**	just, righteous
iuventa -ae, f	youth (2.15)
iuventūs -ūtis, f	youth (4.50, 6.33)
***lābor, labi, lapsus sum**	to collapse
***labor, laboris**, m	toil, labour (4.39)
Lacaena -ae, f	Spartan woman (Helen: 3.25)
lacesso, lacessere, lacessivi, lacessitum	to goad, provoke
***laetus -a -um** (+ ablative)	rejoicing in, delighted with (4.34)
Laomedon, Laomedontis, m	Laomedon (3.22)
***late** (adverb)	far and wide
laurus -i, f	laurel
lavo, lavere/lavare, lāvi/lavavi, lavatum/lautum	to wash
lenis -e	gentle
leo, leonis, m	lion
***lex, legis**, f	law
***libens, libentis**	willing
ligo, ligonis, m	mattock, hoe (6.38)
limen, liminis, n	limit, threshold (4.10)
liquidus -a -um	watery
liquor, liquoris, m	water, sea (3.46)
***litus, litoris**, n	shore, coast
***longus -a -um**	wide (3.37), long (4.2)
lucidus -a -um	light-filled, bright
luctuosus -a -um	sorrowing, grieving (6.8)
lucus -i, m	grove
ludo, ludere, lusi, lusum	to play
ludus -i, m	play
lugubris -e	gloomy, dismal

lumen, luminis, n	light
luo, luere, lui, luitum	to atone for, pay for (6.1)
luridus -a -um	ghastly, sickly-yellow (of the Underworld: 4.74)
Lycia -ae, f	Lycia (4.62)
lyra -ae, f	lyre
maereo, maerere	to mourn for
***magister, magistri,** m	ship's captain (6.31)
***magnus -a -um**	great, large
maiores, maiorum, m.pl.	ancestors
***malo, malle, malui**	to prefer
***malus -a -um**	bad, evil
***manus -ūs,** f	hand (3.6), band of men (6.9)
***mare, maris,** n	the sea
***maritus -i,** m	husband
Mars, Martis, m	Mars (god of war), war (3.16)
masculus -a -um	male
***mater, matris,** f	mother
matrona -ae, f	married woman
maturus -a -um	grown-up (of a girl: 6.22)
***mecum**	with me
***medius -a -um**	the thick of (the fighting: 2.12), in the middle (3.46)
meditor, meditari, meditatus sum	to think about, dream of (6.24)
Medus -i, m	a Mede (3.44)
***melior, melioris**	better (comparative of *bonus*)
melos -i, n	song, melody
***mens, mentis,** f	mind
merces, mercēdis, f	payment, reward

mereor, mereri, meritus sum	to deserve
metuendus -a -um (gerundive of *metuo*)	terrifying
***meus, mea, meum**	my
***miles, militis**, m	soldier
militia -ae, f	army service
Mimas, Mimantis, m	Mimas (a Giant: 6.53)
minax, minacis	threatening
Minerva -ae, f	Minerva (goddess: 3.23)
***minor, minoris** (comparative of *parvus*)	inferior (6.5)
mirus -a -um	amazing, wonderful
missilis -e	flying, shot (of arrows: 6.16)
***mitto, mittere, misi, missum**	to send
***modus -i**, m	measure (i.e. musical or poetic style: 3.72)
***moenia, moenium**, n.pl.	city-walls
moles, molis, f	weight, mass (4.65)
Monaeses, Monaesis, m	Monaeses (Parthian general: 6.9)
***mons, montis**, m	mountain
monstrum -i, n	monster (4.73)
***morior, mori, mortuus sum**	to die
***mors, mortis**, f	death
mortalis -e	mortal, human (4.47)
motus -ūs, m	movement, dance
***moveo, movere, movi, motum**	to move
***mox**	soon
***mulier, mulieris**, f	woman
***multus -a -um**	many
mundus -i, m	world (3.53)
***murus -i**, m	wall

Musa -ae, f	Muse
***muto, mutare, mutavi, mutatum**	to alter, change (6.42)
myrtus -i, f	myrtle
natalis -e	of his birth, native (4.63)
***navis -is**, f	ship
navita -ae, m	sailor
***ne** (conjunction with subjunctive)	so that ... not (2.9, 3.58)
nebula -ae, f	rain-cloud
***nec**	= **neque**
nectar, nectaris, n	nectar (drink of the gods)
nefas, n	wrongdoing, misdeed
***nego, negare, negavi, negatum**	to deny, forbid
***neglego, neglegere, neglexi, neglectum**	to neglect, ignore (2.30)
nepos, nepotis, m	grandson
***neque** (or **nec**)	neither, nor, and not
nequior (comparative of *nequam*)	more wicked
nequitia -ae, f	wickedness
nescius -a um (+ genitive)	knowing nothing of (2.17)
nidus -i, m	nest
niger, nigra, nigrum	black
Nilus -i, m	the river Nile (3.48)
nimium	too much, too
***nomen, nominis**, n	name
***non**	not
***nos, nostri**	we, us
***noster, nostra, nostrum**	our
***notus -a -um**	well-known (4.70)
***novus -a -um**	new
***numquam**	never
***nunc**	now
nuptiae, nuptiarum, f.pl.	marriage, wedding
nutrix, nutricis, f	nurse
obsto, obstare, obstiti, obstatum	to stand as a limit to (3.53)

*occupo, occupare, occupavi, occupatum	to beset, preoccupy (6.13)
*odi, odisse	to hate
Olympus -i, m	Olympus (mountain: 4.52)
*omnis -e	all
opacus -a -um	dark
*oppidum -i, n	town
*ops, opis, f (used in plural)	strength, help (3.28)
*ora -ae, f	shore, coast
orbis -is, m	firmament, heavens (3.7)
Orcus -i, m	Orcus (the Underworld: 4.75)
*ordo, ordinis, m	rank
Orion, Orionis, m	Orion (a hunter: 4.71)
*orior, oriri, ortus sum	to arise, be born from (6.33)
*os, oris, n	mouth
Pacorus -i, m	Pacorus (king of Parthia: 6.9)
pactus -a -um	settled, fixed
*paene	almost
Palinurus -i, m	Cape Palinurus (4.28)
Pallas, Palladis, f	Pallas (Greek name for Minerva: 4.57)
palumbis -is, m/f	wood-pigeon
*parco, parcere, peperci, parsum (+ dative)	to spare
*parens, parentis, m/f	parent
*pario, parere, peperi, partum	to give birth to
Paris, Paridis, m	Paris (son of Priam: 3.26, 3.40)
*pars, partis, f	region (3.39, 3.55)
Parthus -i, m	a Parthian (2.3)
partus -ūs, m	offspring

*parvus -a -um	small
Patareus, -ei	Pataraean (4.64)
*pater, patris, m	father
*patior, pati, passus sum	to allow, suffer
*patria -ae, f	fatherland, native country
pauperies, ei, f	poverty
*peior (comparative of malus) worse	
Pelion -ii, n	Mt Pelion (4.52)
*per (+ accusative)	through
*pereo, perire, peri(v)i, peritum	to perish
perĕdo, perĕdere, perēdi, perēsum	to eat through, consume (4.75)
peregrinus -a -um	foreign
Perithous, Perithoi, m	Pirithous (4.80)
periurus -a -um	treacherous, faithless
persequor, persequi, persecutus sum	to hunt down, chase after
pervicax, pervicacis (adjective)	headstrong
*pes, pedis, m	foot
pharetratus -a -um	armed with a quiver
phaselos -i, m/f	boat
Philippi, -orum, m	Philippi (town in Macedonia: 4.26)
Phoebus -i, m	Phoebus Apollo (3.66, 4.4)
Pierius -a -um	Pierian (i.e. belonging to the Muses: 4.40)
pinguis -e	rich (of earth: 4.16)
pinna -ae, f	wing
pius -a -um	pious, dutiful (3.58), holy (4.6)
*placeo, placere, placui, placitum (+ dative)	to be pleasing to (4.24)

ploro, plorare, ploravi, ploratum	to weep for
pluvius -a um	rainy
Poena -ae, f	Retribution (2.32)
Pollux, Pollūcis, m	Pollux (3.9)
***pono, ponere, posui, positum**	to put down (2.19), to put (4.60)
pontus -i, m	the sea
poples, poplitis, m	hamstring (back of the knee: 2.16)
popularis -e	of the people
***populus -i**, m	the people
Porphyrion, Porphyrionis, m	Porphyrion (a giant: 4.54)
***porto, portare, portavi, portatum**	to carry
***possum, posse, potui**	to be able
***praeda -ae**, f	plunder, booty
Praeneste -is, n	Praeneste (city: 4.23)
pravus -a -um	crooked
premo, premere, pressi, pressum	to cover, protect (4.18)
pretiosus -a -um	lavish, prodigal (of a buyer: 6.32)
Priamus -i, m	Priam (king of Troy: 3.26, 3.40)
primum (adverb)	first of all, firstly
principium -ii, n	beginning
***pro** (+ ablative)	on behalf of
progenies, progeniei, f	offspring
proles -is, f	offspring
propositum -i, n	purpose, aim
prospicio, prospicere, prospexi, prospectum	to gaze out at
protinus (adverb)	henceforth, from now on (3.30)

proveho, provehere, provexi, provectum	to promote
*puer, pueri, m	boy
pugnax, pugnacis	warlike
pulvis, pulveris, m	dust
Punicus -a -um	Carthaginian (6.34)
purpureus -a -um	dark red, rosy (of lips: 3.12)
purus -a -um	pure, clear
Pyrrhus -i, m	Pyrrhus (king of Epirus: 6.35)
quā	where
*quaero, quaerere, quaesivi, quaesitum	to seek, look for
*quam	than
quatio, quatere, (*no perfect*), **quassum**	to shake
*qui, quae, quod	who, which
quicumque, quaecumque, quodcumque	whoever, whatever
*quies, quietis, f	rest
quilibet, quaelibet, quodlibet	any … whatsoever (3.38)
Quirinus -i, m	Romulus (3.15)
Quirites, Quirit(i)um, m.pl.	Roman citizens (3.57)
*quis, quid	who? what?
*quo?	to where?
*quod (conjunction)	because
*quoque	also
*rapio, rapere, rapui, raptum	to drive, whirl (2.12), to snatch, grab (3.52)
raptim (adverb)	hastily (6.27)
raro (adverb)	seldom (2.31)
recīdo, recīdere, recīdi, recīsum	to cut down
recludo, recludere, reclusi, reclusum	to open, unlock
recreo, recreare, recreavi, recreatum	to refresh
recumbo, recumbere, recubui	to recline (on a couch: 3.11)

redono, redonare, redonavi (+ acc. and dat.)	to forgive (3.33)
***refero, referre, rettuli, relatum**	to retell (3.71), to ascribe, derive (6.6)
***reficio, reficere, refeci, refectum**	to rebuild, restore
refringo, refringere, refregi, refractum	to beat back
***regina -ae**, f	queen
regius, regia, regium	royal
regno, regnare, regnavi, regnatum	to reign, rule
***regnum -i**, n	kingdom
***rego, regere, rexi, rectum**	to rule
***relinquo, relinquere, reliqui, relictum**	to leave, abandon (4.78)
removeo, removere, remōvi, remōtum	to remove
renascor, renasci, renatus sum	to rise again, be reborn
renideo, renidere	to grin
reparo, reparare, reparavi, reparatum	to rebuild
repulsa -ae, f	electoral defeat (2.17)
***res, rei**, f	matter, circumstances
resido, residere, resēdi	to subside
resurgo, resurgere, resurrexi, resurrectum	to rise again
retro	backwards
Rhoetus, -i	Rhoetus (a Giant: 4.55)
rigo, rigare, rigavi, rigatum	to flood, irrigate
robustus -a -um	strong, sturdy
Roma -ae, f	Rome
Romanus, -a -um	Roman
ros, roris, m	dew
rudis -e (+ genitive)	unskilled in, with no experience of
ruo, ruere, rui, ruitum	to rush against (4.58), to collapse (4.65)
ruina -ae, f	ruins, debris (in plural: 3.8)

rusticus -a -um	rural, from the countryside
Sabellus -a -um	Sabine, Samnite (6.38)
Sabinus -a -um	Sabine (4.22)
sacer, sacra, sacrum	holy, sacred
*sacerdos, sacerdotis, m/f	priest, priestess
saeculum -i, n	generation, age, century
*saepe	often
saevio, saevire, saevii, saevitum	to rage
sagitta -ae, f	arrow
saltus, -ūs, m	glade
*sanguis, sanguinis, m	blood
scelestus -a -um	guilty, wicked
*scio, scire, scivi, scitum	to know
Scythicus -a -um	Scythian (4.36)
secerno, secernere, secrevi, secretum	to separate, divide
securis -is, f	axe
*sed	but
*sedes -is, f	abode
seditio, seditionis, f	faction-fighting, civil discord (3.29)
*sententia -ae, f	opinion
sermo, sermonis, m	talk, conversation
*seu ... seu	whether ... or
severus -a -um	strict
*si	if
*sic	thus, in this way
Siculus -a -um	Sicilian
silentium -i, n	silence
*silva -ae, f	wood, forest
*simul	as soon as (4.37)
simulacrum -i, n	image, statue
*sine	without

situs -a um	placed, hidden (3.49)
*sol, solis, m	the sun
solidus -a -um	firm
*solvo, solvere, solvi, solutum	to loose (hair 4.62), to launch (boat 2.29)
*somnus -i, m	sleep
sono, sonare, sonavi, sonatum	to sound
sordidus -a -um	dirty, disgraceful
*soror, sororis, f	sister
*sperno, spernere, sprēvi, sprētum	to reject, spurn
splendeo, splendere	to show off (3.25)
sponsus -i, m	fiancé, bridegroom
status -ūs, m	stance (fighting pose: 4.54)
*sto, stare, steti, statum	to stand
*sub + ablative	under
*subeo, subire, subi(v)i, subitum	to penetrate, go down into
sucus -i, m	juice, flavour
*sum, esse, fui	to be
*sumo, sumere, sumpsi, sumptum	to take up
supinus -a -um	sloping down, lying flat
*surgo, surgere, surrexi, surrectum	to rise, arise
suspiro, suspirare, suspiravi, suspiratum	to sigh
sustulerit	see **tollo**
*suus, -a -um	his own, her own, its own, their own
*tango, tangere, tetigi, tactum	to touch
*tectum, -i, n	house
*tego, tegere, texi, tectum	to cover
tempero, temperare, temperavi, temperatum	to control (of Jupiter: 4.45)

*templum -i, n	temple
temptator, -oris, m	assailant, attacker
tempto, temptare, temptavi, temptatum	to attempt
*tempus, temporis, n	time, hour
tenax, tenacis (+ genitive)	holding on to (3.1)
tendo, tendere, tetendi, tensum	to go (3.70), to strive (+ infinitive: 4.51)
*teneo, tenere, tenui, tentum	to hold, occupy
tener, -a, -um	young, delicate (used figuratively: 6.24)
tenuo, tenuare, tenuavi, tenuatum	to make thin, to diminish
ter (adverb)	three times
*tergum -i, n	back
terminus -i, m	boundary, limit (3.53)
*terra -ae, f	land
*terror, -oris, m	alarm, fear
testis -is, m/f	witness
tibia -ae, f	pipe (musical instrument)
Tibur, -uris, n	Tivoli (a town: 4.23)
tigris -is, m	tiger
timidus -a -um	timid, fearful
Titan, Titanis	a Titan (4.43)
Tityos, Tityi, m	Tityos (a Giant: 4.77)
*tollo, tollere, sustuli, sublatum	to eliminate, carry off (4.44)
*tollor (passive of *tollo*)	to climb (4.22)
torquis -is, m/f	neckband, ornamental collar
trabs, trabis, f	roof-beam
*traho, trahere, traxi, tractum	to pull, draw (3.15)
trecenti -ae -a	three hundred
trepidus -a -um	agitated, anxious
*tristis -e	grim (3.62), gloomy, sad (4.46)

triumpho, triumphare, triumphavi, triumphatum	to triumph over
Troia -ae, f	Troy (3.60–1)
Troicus -a -um	Trojan
truncus -i, m	tree-trunk
***tu, tui**	you (singular)
***tulit**	see **fero**
tumidus -a -um	swelling, swollen
***turba -ae**, f	mob, crowd
turbidus -a -um	wild, stormy, rebellious (3.5)
turma -ae, f	squadron, troop
***tutus -a -um**	safe
***tuus -a -um**	your
Typhoeus, -eos, m	Typhoeus (a Giant: 4.53)
tyrannus -i, m	tyrant
***ubi**	when, where
udus -a -um	moist, damp
***ultimus -a -um**	furthest, most remote
umbra -ae, f	shadow
umerus -i, m	shoulder
***unda -ae**, f	wave, waters
unguis -is, m	fingernail (used figuratively: 6.24)
***unus -a -um**	alone, one
***urbs, urbis**, f	city
uro, urere, ussi, ustum	to burn
ursus -i, m	bear
***ūsus -ūs**, m	use (3.51)
***ut**	so that (4.17–18), how (4.42)
utcumque	whenever
***uxor, uxoris**, f	wife
vagus -a -um	roaming, travelling

*validus -a -um	strong, mighty
*veho, vehere, vexi, vectum	to transport, carry, bring
ventosus -a -um	windy
verso, versare, versavi, versatum	to turn over
*verto, vertere, verti, versum	to turn around, to rout
*vester, vestra, vestrum	your
*veto, vetare, vetui, vetitum	to forbid
vexo, vexare, vexavi, vexatum	to harass, trouble
*via -ae, f	road, path
viator, viatoris, m	traveller
victrix, victricis	conquering, victorious
*videor, videri, visus sum	to seem
vinum -i, n	wine
vipera -ae, f	viper, snake
*vir, viri, m	man
*vires, virium, f	force, power
virgineus -a -um	girlish, virgin
virgo, virginis, f	virgin, unmarried girl
*virtus, virtutis, f	manliness, courage, virtue
*vis (no genitive)	force, violence
viso, visere, visi, visum	to visit, to go to see
*vita -ae, f	life
vitiosus -a -um	wicked
*voco, vocare, vocavi, vocatum	to call
*volo, velle, volui	to want
*vos, vestrum	you (plural)
*vox, vocis, f	voice
Vulcanus -i, m	Vulcan (god of fire: 4.59)
vulgaris -e	common, vulgar
vulgo, vulgare, vulgavi, vulgatum	to make public
Vultur, Vulturis, m	Vultur (mountain: 4.9)
*vultus -ūs, m	face, facial expression